Then and Now
On the Crowd, the Subject, and the Collective

THE SEA HORSE IMPRINT

Paola Mieli, *Publisher & Director*
Mark Stafford, *Editorial Director*
David Jacobson, Ona Nierenberg, and Peter Gillespie, *Supporting Editors*

This book is published under the aegis and with the financial assistance of
Après-Coup Psychoanalytic Association, New York
and
with the financial support of The Solomon and Gillespie Fund

Cover Image: AI-enhanced reproduction of *Folla* (Crowd)
by Guglielmo Sansoni (Tato), 1942

Betty Bernardo Fuks, Paola Mieli, Rosalind Morris,
David Pavón-Cuéllar, Alain Vanier

Then and Now

On the Crowd, the Subject, and the Collective

Agincourt Press
New York, 2024

ISBN: 978-1-946328-48-9

Copyediting
Hilary Ilkay

Design and typesetting
Danilo Montanari

Agincourt Press
P.O. Box 1039
Cooper Station
New York, NY 10003
www.agincourtbooks.com

The publisher welcomes enquiries from copyright-holders he has been unable to contact.

Table of Contents

Introduction
Paola Mieli

The present volume gathers together the reflections of different authors on the nature of the crowd, the collective, and the subject's relation to the social link. These reflections have been written over the last three years, since the centenary of Freud's *Group Psychology and Analysis of the Ego*, published in 1921, an anniversary that took place at a moment of extreme political and social distress for our world, plunged, moreover, into a pandemic that inevitably recalled the famous "Spanish flu" epidemic of 1918-20, which infected an estimated 500 million globally and killed 50 million.[1]

Freud lost his daughter Sophie to it; she died far from him, in Hamburg, on January 25, 1920. Writing to Oskar Pfister about his loss, he added the following comment: "The undisguised brutality of our time is weighing heavily upon us."[2] Unfortunately, this comment rings true for our current reality.

Of course, times are different and, as Rosalind Morris emphasizes in her essay, "the task of historical analysis is to grasp the apparent repetitions as occasions for making the past illuminate the present, not only in its origins and thus as continuities, but in its differences."[3] Looking at the events that transformed Western political dynamics with World War I, we may wonder to what degree those transformations ushered in an era in which we are still inscribed. Exploring its premises and reflecting on figures who took part in it is a fertile ground for understanding the present ramifications of a common history.

David Pavón-Cuéllar maps out here how the collapse of the German, Russian, and Austro-Hungarian empires gave way to aspira-

---

[1] On December 30, 2023, the estimated number of global deaths for Covid-19 was 6,727,216.

[2] Freud, letter to Oskar Pfister of January 27, 1920, in *Letters of Sigmund Freud, Selected and Edited by Ernst Freud 1873-1939*, Dover Publications, New York, 1960, p. 338.

[3] See below, p. 79.

tions toward democratic regimes, and how the ensuing revolutionary uprisings brought to the fore a passion for equality, for fraternal alliance opposed to imperial fatherhood. He approaches these events as a sign of the general waning of paternal power, a decline that Lacan in 1938—a year fraught with political significance—associated with the appearance of psychoanalysis itself. Indeed, some twenty years later, Lacan underscored that if our time follows Nietzsche's proclamation of God's death, the very fact of such a proclamation paved the way for Freud's invention of the myth of the murder of the primordial father: *"peut-être le seul mythe dont l'époque moderne ait été capable,"*[4] "perhaps the only myth the modern era could come up with."

Questioning the paternalistic structure that for centuries has controlled power and the systems of production through its division of the sexes, classes, and roles (both precapitalistic and capitalistic) has never ceased to be part of an epistemology which reflects it. Yet some thinkers, and Freud in particular, devised from within such an epistemology essential tools for analyzing its logic and studying its facets, thereby tracing viable paths toward its possible deconstruction—a project still underway. Begun in the wake of the great revolutions of the late 18th century, this process moved slowly but resolutely, sometimes taking one step forward and two steps back, depending on political contexts and the evolution of the capitalist discourse. This is not surprising, since it was attempting to wrest free from a logic and hegemony that has dominated Western culture for millennia. It is important therefore not to draw hasty conclusions; indeed, we are urged not to do so in view of the current neo-liberal system, which perversely swallows up many egalitarian openings through new forms of alienation and exploitation. For this reason, it is worthwhile not to abandon reflecting, as the authors in the present volume, each in their way, have committed themselves to do.

"*...Au depart le père est mort. Seulement voilà, il reste le Nom-du-Père et tout tourne autour de cela,*"[5] "First the father is dead. Only,

---

[4] J. Lacan, *L'éthique de la psychanalyse, Le séminaire Livre VII*, Éditions du Seuil, Paris, 1986, p. 208. The fact that such a myth is a "neurotic product" does not take away the truth of its construction: "c'est meme en cela qu'elle est temoignage de la verité," "indeed it's for that reason that this construction attests to the truth," J. Lacan, *D'un discours qui ne serait pas du semblant, Le séminaire Livre XVIII*, Éditions du Seuil, Paris, 2006, p. 161.

[5] J. Lacan, *D'un Autre à l'autre, Le séminaire Livre XVI*, Éditions du Seuil, Paris, 2006, p. 151.

lo and behold, the Name of the Father remains, and everything re-
volves around that," Lacan observes, devoting much of his teaching to
examining and deconstructing that Name of the Father in its subjective and collective implications. If psychoanalysis has to reckon with
this, it's because its advent is of a piece with the progress of modern
science. Modern science develops along the way paved by Descartes,
extrapolating God the Father from the world. As a necessary but external reference point, God is the guarantor of both eternal and revealed
truths. This opens the way to the study of natural laws, freeing inves-
tigators from the responsibility of their own discoveries. According to
Lacan, the advent of psychoanalysis is of a piece with the expulsion of
truth from the dialectic of the subject and knowledge; truth returns in
the form of symptoms, in subjective and collective suffering, the echo
of an unassimilable, inexhaustible real which the *parlêtre*, the human
speaking subject, can't cease to confront. This intrinsically binds psychoanalysis to science and to the various articulations of its discourse
in current systems of production.

    David Pavón Cuéllar offers a fertile examination of how a se-
ries of crucial 20th-century authors interpreted the crowd, stressing
the radical difference between a pyramidal vision of the group and
an egalitarian one that disrupts the logic of patriarchy. He posits two
kinds of masses, with two different origins and foundations, depending on either patriarchal or matriarchal logic, in an evident wish to establish a collectivity animated by a productive brotherhood—of which
Rosa Luxemburg was an exceptional advocate. In this way he raises a
question that runs throughout the present volume: How to relaunch a
bond of community that respects differences and takes responsibility
for social well-being, a need that seems increasingly urgent (yet that
also seems increasingly unachievable) in these dark times marked by
both new forms of totalitarianism and the individualistic breakdown
of a sense of the collective. Within this framework, it's worth pointing
out that for Freud the notion of *Massen* refers to a specific social and
libidinal formation, exemplified by the Church and the Army, a formation that aspires to the One and that differs from other collective
forms, precisely those that include and recognize the *not-all*. This is
a question I attempt to develop in my own contribution by returning
to the fascination with the One as studied by Étienne de La Boétie in
the mid-16th century and by Freud. It is precisely the dimension of the
"collective," based, as it is, on an experience of dis-identification and

listening to one's own subjective division (as differentiated from that of the mass), that can open up a fertile social space, inclusive of the real and of difference, in opposition to the promise of an imaginary completeness founded upon the exclusion of what is other. From this standpoint, a psychoanalysis worthy of the name can make essential contributions.

In going back over key elements of the complex and intricate historical reality of South African white supremacism before Apartheid, Rosalind Morris closely follows the ambiguous and emblematic career of the expatriate South African literary figure Roy Campbell, shedding light on crucial aspects of the way in which early progressivism could turn into segregationism. She recalls, among other things, how in the 1920s the white working class became "the popular base for a resurgent Afrikaner nationalism whose final victory in 1948 opened onto the formalization and constitutionalization of Stallardist principles of segregation in the form of Apartheid."[6] In a way that may remind readers of Paul Gilroy's expression "postcolonial melancholia," Morris explores the facets of white supremacist melancholia, an affect that continues to have a political impact on contemporary life, metapsychologically organized as it is in libidinal investment of the (lost) Ideal and the One. Returning to Walter Benjamin's analysis on the Left's attachment to vanished spiritual values when confronted with change, as well as to Adorno's thoughts on the "secularization of melancholy," she also calls into question the melancholia of the liberal critics of racism and white nationalism, and the harmful blocking effects such a melancholia produces. The need to elaborate a conceptual infrastructure for the collective "without, at the same time, submitting to the lure of the one,"[7] remains urgent.

Repetition inscribes difference; it's always repetition in difference. Occasionally, its figures can be surprising if not stunning. This is also the case when in a new context one intentionally adopts outrageous solutions from the past. Betty Fuks's essay illustrates a literal adoption of some key terms from Nazi propaganda by Bolsonaro and members of his government. Involved here is a choice which, unlikely as it may seem, is not far from languages familiar to us and prompts reflection both upon the nature of the language under totalitarianism,

---

[6] See below, p. 57.
[7] See below, p. 83.

then and now, and upon the shamelessness with which society today appropriates expressions associated with racism and genocide. Yet more than "association" is in play here: Fuks reminds us of Gustave Le Bon's insistence that words are "living things"; for the *parlêtre*, the word, as Franz Rosenzweig remarked, "is more than blood." It is not by chance that psychoanalysis was born as a 'talking cure,' centered precisely upon the nature of language in the psyche, a cure in language that radically differed from suggestion and all the practices close to it. Except that another side of the power of language is precisely its use for manipulation and seduction; it is suggestion, something that the tyrants of all eras have always been aware of, and that both 20th-century totalitarianism and the marketing and public relations practice of Freud's own nephew, Mr. Edward Bernays, made into a gospel and a science—emulated by the "influencers" of our own moment. If adulteration of language was one of the most important means to reform German identity in the Nazi era, as Fuks stresses, the question remains not only that of the adoption of these formulae by totalitarian states, but also the adoption of the same protocols by media marketing, by post-deconstructionist ideologies and telematic psychotherapies—all forms of repetition in difference working toward new enslavements and new alienations.

As obsolete as it may seem, the function of the Name of the Father in current-day aspects of capitalist discourse continues to warrant attention. Lacan notes that the myth of the death of the primal father "is testimony that obsessives produce out of their own structure, inasmuch as the sexual relation proves to be impossible."[8] In his contribution to the present volume, Alain Vanier returns to the archaeology of the category of obsessional neurosis, highlighting its specific drive structure, as Freud came to identify it. More than other neuroses, Vanier emphasizes, obsessional neurosis reveals the contemporary paradox of the father. In constructing the figure of "the obsessive," a fictitious envelope that each case will inhabit differently, Vanier traces the drive profile of the characteristic neurosis of modern times, which, freeing itself from the father, doesn't cease to appeal to the father and give him solid embodiment. He underlines the delusion of autonomy that Lacan considered characteristic of our era, the idea of being a

---

[8] J. Lacan, *D'un discours qui ne serait pas du semblant*, op. cit, p. 161.

subject without Other. Rooted in the myth of individualism and in the constant claims for individual freedom, the delusion of the autonomy of the ego represents in his view "a return to the discourse of the Master," "a twist of the capitalist's discourse to re-establish the Master's discourse."[9] Under the auspices of so-called "individual freedom," the promise of which animates both progressive identity discourses and racist, supremacist, and totalitarian discourses (a common currency of today's neoliberal modes of production) are parceled out new forms of segregation and new biopolitical manipulations.

We have every reason, then, to roll up our sleeves and press our study on past and current forms of voluntary servitude. In this sense it seemed useful to go back to La Boétie and to the crucial question Freud raised in the wake of his dialog with jurist Hans Kelsen: what leads us to obey, what keeps us from rebelling against constraints? Freud's reflections on the nature of the Superego, as well as those of Lacan on the structure of the divided subject and the logic of the not-all, offer a path that remains fertile for thinking about new forms of the relation between subject and collective.

---

[9] See below, p. 117.

Sons and Brothers: Two Kinds of Mass Psychology
David Pavón-Cuéllar

The Collapse of Empires and the Crisis of Paternity

The German, Russian, Austro-Hungarian, and Ottoman empires collapsed almost simultaneously between 1917 and 1918 at the end of World War I. In a few months, old institutions that seemed eternal gave way to democratic regimes and revolutionary uprisings. It was a time not only of the Weimar Republic and Red Vienna, but also of the October Revolution, the establishment of the Soviet Union, the Republic of Councils in Hungary, the Bavarian Soviet Republic, and the Berlin Commune. In all cases, the passion for equality and against hierarchies spread.

The imperial fatherhood of the tsar, the sultan, and the kaiser was abolished and replaced by the republican fraternity, which sometimes took a social democratic, socialist, and even communist form. It is as if the brothers had triumphed over a father figure who later returned in some way, symbolized in figures such as Kemal, Stalin, Hitler, or Dollfuss. All this irresistibly reminds us of what Sigmund Freud recounts in *Totem and Taboo* about the end of the primordial horde, when the brothers killed and devoured their father, "and in the act of devouring him they accomplished their identification with him, and each one of them acquired a portion of his strength."[1] The all-powerful primitive father was eventually resurrected in the patriarchal leaders, but before that, there was a moment of equality and fraternity.

In the Freudian account of the origin of civilization, as in Europe between the wars, parricide was the triumph of "social fraternal feelings" and their expressions in "democratic equality."[2] However, this led to "the revenge taken by the deposed and restored father" through

---

[1] S. Freud, *Totem and Taboo*, Routledge, London, 2001, p. 165.
[2] *Ibid.*, pp. 169, 172.

tyrants who "introduced the patriarchal system into the state."[3] This was the glorious moment of *Ata-Türk*, the Turk father, as well as Stalinism, Fascism, and Nazism.

Something in the European history of the first third of the 20th century manifested in the aforementioned events and through Freudian thought. This was perhaps the "social decadence of the paternal imago," with which the young Jacques Lacan hypothetically explained "the appearance of psychoanalysis."[4] Freud would have conceived of the Oedipus Complex, as well as its prehistoric projection in the primordial horde, under the influence of the paternity crisis that appeared in hysteria and history, in the patients of the Viennese doctor and the collapse of the empires and the revolutionary masses.

Lacan seems to have found the notion of a fading father figure in the work of Émile Durkheim.[5] The French sociologist had observed in 1892 that the modern nuclear family stems from a development in which there is not only a contraction of the family but also an individualization of its members and an erosion of the authority of the father. Among the signs of this erosion are the appearance of a "sphere of action" of each member of the family, the "narrow limitation" of the "disciplinary power of the father," and the exclusive right of the state—and no longer of the father—to maintain or break kinship ties.[6]

Federn: Between the Patriarchal Society and the Collective Fraternity

The decline of old paternal power is the historical factor by which Lacan in 1938 explains the appearance of psychoanalysis. Regardless of whether we accept this explanation, we must at least acknowledge that the weakening of paternity is crucial to everything studied by psychoanalysis. This was well appreciated not only by Lacan in 1938 but

---

[3] *Ibid.*, p. 174.

[4] J. Lacan, "Les complexes familiaux dans la formation de l'individu" (1938), in *Autres écrits*, Éditions du Seuil, Paris, 2001, p. 61.

[5] M. Zafiropoulos, "Le déclin du père," *Topique*, 84 (3), 2003, pp. 161-171.

[6] É. Durkheim, "La Famille conjugale" (1892), *Revue Philosophique de la France et de l'Étranger* 46, 1921, pp. 3-4.

also, some twenty years before, by Paul Federn, who in 1919 devoted a lecture to the question of the crisis of the father figure.[7]

Examining the revolutionary situation at the end of the war in Europe, Federn noted the symbolic paternal role of imperial monarchs and interpreted their dethronement as signifying the decline of paternity. Federn explained this historical change by the discrediting of the emperors, who ruthlessly immolated their "sons" on battlefronts.[8] The result was that the people experienced during the war "the same disappointment toward their fathers" that they had felt at the time of the resolution of the Oedipus Complex.[9]

Parallel to the disappointment with imperial father figures, another process attracted Federn's attention: the development of workers' class consciousness. This process allowed each subject to "get rid of the affective bond" with the paternal figures of their oppressors and exploiters.[10] In some cases, the rise of class consciousness led to the cult of personality of communist leaders. In other cases, "the desire for liberation with respect to the father was so strong" that it gave rise to workers' councils "built on the collective fraternity." The best example of this fraternal form of organization was the Spartacist Uprising in Berlin.

Federn recognizes the decisive historical crossroads whereby the socialist project forks into two paths. One path returns to the horde, that is, the rebirth of the primordial father and the reconstitution of power in the form of party leaders, be it in the tradition of the European social democracy or of Soviet Marxism-Leninism. The other path, which travels through Spartacism and leads to council communism, takes the crisis of paternity to its ultimate consequences, creating an egalitarian movement founded on the "fraternal psychic structure" and potentially linked to the "matriarchy."[11] This second path has one of its first reflective justifications in the socialist doctrine of Rosa Luxemburg.

---

[7] P. Federn, "De la psychologie de la révolution: la société sans père" (1919), *Essaim* 5, 2000, pp. 153-173.

[8] *Ibid.*, pp. 160-161.

[9] *Ibid.*, p. 161.

[10] *Ibid.*, pp. 159-160.

[11] *Ibid.*, pp. 163-164.

Luxemburg: Equality in the School of History

The Marxist theoretician and communist militant Rosa Luxemburg questioned the Leninist strategy of the party's revolutionary vanguard leading the masses. For Luxemburg, this strategy reproduced the "slave discipline" inculcated by the capitalist state.[12] Instead of a leadership outside the masses, the Luxemburgian proposal is the "voluntary self-discipline" of the masses as a foreshadowing of a socialist society.[13] For Luxemburg, the masses must direct themselves.

The first Luxemburgian strategic principle is the "conscious self-determination" of the masses.[14] This self-determination is already the freedom for which the masses are fighting. They must conquer it not at the end of their struggle but before, when they are fighting in the councils and their other radically democratic, horizontal, and egalitarian forms of organization. Thus, the struggle of the masses can also immediately offer them the equality for which they are fighting. This equality is already realized in the fraternal relationships of the communist movement, which challenges any filial submission to the symbolic paternity of community party leaders.

Once the masses come to power, as they did in Russia in 1917, the government must be prevented from being taken over by the party leadership. The dictatorship of the proletariat must be "the work of the class and not of a small minority of leaders in the name of the class."[15] Socialism must be the government of the masses and does not require any mediation by leaders outside of them.

In the Luxemburgian vision, the masses do not require the paternal function of those who "act as teachers," since "revolutions are not learned in school," but in the revolutionary struggle, itself, as a "living school of events."[16] It is history, not the Marxist intelligentsia, that has something to teach the masses. In Lacanian terms, the discourse

---

[12] R. Luxemburg, "Problemas de organización de la socialdemocracia rusa" (1904), in *Obras escogidas*, Ayuso, Madrid, 1978, p. 37.

[13] *Ibid.*, pp. 36-41.

[14] R. Luxemburg, "¿Qué se propone la Liga Espartaco?" (1918), in *Obras escogidas*, Ayuso, Madrid, 1978, p. 152.

[15] R. Luxemburg, *Crítica de la Revolución Rusa* (1918), La Rosa Blindada, Buenos Aires, 1969, p. 128.

[16] R. Luxemburg, "Huelga de masas, partido y sindicatos" (1905), in *Obras escogidas*, Ayuso, Madrid, 1978, pp. 53-63.

of the masses must not be the modern discourse of the master, the university discourse that Lacan associated with Marxism-Leninism,[17] but the discourse of history, of hysteria, which we can attribute to Rosa Luxemburg.[18]

The Luxemburgian discursive strategy returns power to the subjects, finds this power in the truth of their desire, and allows them to question their masters and, hence, produce knowledge. For Luxemburg, only the masses "know" what is at stake in a specific context, and that is why the best initiatives "arise spontaneously from the masses."[19] It is for the same reason that the masses must "give a clear objective and direction to the revolution."[20] The revolutionary movement must have no compass other than the masses.

Freud: Resurrected Horde in the Masses

The Luxemburgian conception of the masses is diametrically opposed to the one that Freud seems to propose in *Group Psychology and Analysis of the Ego*. This work, planned a few months after the murder of Rosa Luxemburg in January 1919 and written in the following two years, contains serious objections to the Luxemburgian viewpoint. Freud's text also challenges much of what Federn elaborated on in his aforementioned text, also from 1919.

While Federn and Luxemburg admit the possibility of a fraternal and horizontal mass configuration, Freud excludes this possibility and attributes to groups a necessarily vertical structure based on filial relationships with paternal leadership figures. This structure, which Luxemburg strives to overcome and which Federn hopes to see overcome in communist councils, appears insurmountable in Freud's theory of the masses. It is impossible to overcome it because the human being, according to Freud, is not a "herd animal," but a "horde animal, an

---

[17] J. Lacan, *L'envers de la psychanalyse, Le séminaire Livre XVII*, Éditions du Seuil, Paris, 1991, pp. 34-37.

[18] J. Lacan, *Le moment de conclure, Le séminaire Livre XXV*, Association Freudienne Internationale, Paris, 2002, p. 31.

[19] R. Luxemburg, "El orden reina en Berlín" (1919), in *La Comuna de Berlín*, Grijalbo, Mexico City, 1971, p. 73.

[20] R. Luxemburg, "¿Qué se propone la Liga Espartaco?", *op. cit.*, p. 152.

individual creature in a horde led by a chief."[21] This horde, the eternal prehistoric horde of *Totem and Taboo*, revives in the modern masses, which, consequently, again shows the vertical structure of the horde, "the familiar picture of an individual of superior strength among a troop of equal companions."[22]

Federn and Luxemburg hoped that equal comrades would succeed in freeing themselves from the yoke of the strong individual. For Freud, this liberation would endanger the very subsistence of the masses, since, for him, "the mutual ties between the members of the group disappear, as a rule, at the same time as the tie with their leader."[23] For Freud, even egalitarian fraternity originates in the bond with the leader.

A fundamental Freudian hypothesis is that love for the leader awakens among a crowd deep feelings of rivalry, jealousy, and envy, similar to those that arise in childhood between siblings in their relationship with their father. However, these feelings, for one reaction formation, become their opposite, a "group spirit," in which "no one must want to put himself forward, everyone must be the same and have the same."[24] Freud finds here the foundation of social justice, which means to him that "we deny ourselves many things so that others may have to do without them as well."[25] It is revealing that this typically Hobbesian liberal and individualist idea served Freud to explain the "demand for equality."[26]

For Freud, the egalitarian demand of the communists, especially Rosa Luxemburg, would not be more than a petty expression of the original rivalry between the brothers in their relationship with the father. The lack of the paternal figure of the leader would undermine the very foundation of equality, since the equality inherent in fraternal relationships would be based on the inequality proper to the filial bond with the father. The horde animals could associate horizontally because they would submit vertically to the father of the horde.

---

[21] S. Freud, "Group Psychology and the Analysis of the Ego," in *The Standard Edition of the Complete Psychological Works, Vol. XVIII (1920-1922): Beyond the Pleasure Principle, Group Psychology and Other Works*, The Hogarth Press, London, 1955, p. 120.

[22] *Ibid.*, p. 121.

[23] *Ibid.*, p. 96.

[24] *Ibid.*, p. 119.

[25] *Ibid.*, p. 120.

[26] *Ibid.*

According to Freud, "the group still wishes to be governed by the unrestricted force" of the "dreaded primal father."[27] This force gives cohesion to the group by unifying it under the single force of the leader, his power and his will, the group's love for him, and his being as an ideal shared by the entire group. Therefore, the Freudian conceptualization of the group coincides with Hobbes's idea of the people as "somewhat that is one, having one will,"[28] which clearly distinguishes it from "the multitude not yet reduced into one Person," in which "all things belong to all men"[29] and "the natural equality of men" reigns.[30] This multitude, which corresponds to the communist masses for Luxembourg and Federn, was repudiated by Hobbes and had to wait for Baruch Spinoza to be revalued and repositioned with its "*potentia*"[31] at the foundation of the people and any kind of "power."[32]

Self-abolition of Leadership: From the Primordial Horde to the Spartacist Movement

This conceptualization of the group united by its leader is not Freud's original idea but rather a widespread belief that recurs in history. Due to this belief, governments of all times have sought to eliminate the leaders of opposition movements to cause a rout among their followers. It happened in January 1919, when the proto-fascist paramilitaries of the *Freikorps*, then working for the Social Democratic government of Friedrich Ebert, executed Rosa Luxemburg and Karl Liebknecht on the grounds that they were the ringleaders of the Spartacist revolt.

The person directly responsible for the execution of Luxemburg and Liebknecht, Captain Waldemar Pabst, explained simply, "The two were the spiritual leaders of the revolution, and I decided to have them killed."[33] Their leadership justified their murder, which is paradoxical,

---

[27] *Ibid.*, p. 120.
[28] T. Hobbes, *De Cive* (1652), Oxford University Press, New York, 1983, pp. 151-152.
[29] *Ibid.*, p. 91.
[30] *Ibid.*, p. 45.
[31] B. Spinoza, *Traité théologico-politique* (1670), GF-Gallimard, Paris, 1965, p. 277.
[32] B. Spinoza, *Traité politique* (1675), GF-Gallimard, Paris, 1966, pp. 58-19.
[33] Quoted by Nicolás González Varela, "Un cadáver en el canal: el Asesinato de

since Luxemburg wanted to shake off individual leadership. The paradox seems even greater when we consider that Luxemburg did not agree with the revolt that cost her life but supported it resolutely precisely because of her resolution to side with the masses, renouncing any individual power in favor of collective self-determination.

Luxemburg had power over the Spartacists, of course, but only to suppress it. Accordingly, her spiritual leadership was realized to its last consequences by abolishing itself in a sacrifice that ended with her death. Such power is no longer exactly power but something else: courage, strength, and multitudinous *potentia*. If so, the communist movement demonstrated that it could differ completely from a horde, as imagined by Freud and well understood by Federn.

Luxemburg and Liebknecht confirmed that Federn was right. They demonstrated this by dying like the other Spartacists, since the *Freikorps* savagely massacred not only those identified as leaders but also hundreds of grassroots militants. There was no distinction between the methods of killing. The deaths were as brutal and demeaning for the leaders as for the others, not because death acted as the usual great leveler but because the victims were already leveled before dying.

Knowing the Masses From Within

The actions against the Spartacists had a high material cost partially paid by the industrial magnate and leftist liberal Walther Rathenau. Just three years after the 1919 massacres, Rathenau was assassinated by a branch of the *Freikorps*, the Consul Organization. This anti-communist, anti-Semitic organization chose its former sponsor as a victim for being Jewish, leftist, and a minister of the Weimar Republic, and for having signed a treaty of mutual collaboration with the Soviet Union.

After being a victim of his beneficiaries, Rathenau was mourned by his victims. Tens of thousands of communist workers, like those massacred in 1919 with his financial support, attended his funeral in June 1922 and protested his death in various German cities. In Frankfurt, future Nobel Prize winner Elias Canetti witnessed protest. This

---

Rosa Luxemburgo," *Viento Sur*, October 15, 2019, https://vientosur.info/un-cadaver-en-el-canal-el-asesinato-de-rosa-luxemburgo/.

experience left an indelible mark on Canetti, who became obsessed with the phenomenon of the masses, working for more than three decades on his monumental *Crowds and Power*.[34]

In 1924, two years after his first experience with the masses in Frankfurt, Canetti read Freud's group psychology. He found it "incongruous and unsatisfactory."[35] The problem for Canetti was that Freud, who was only familiar with isolated individuals, studied the masses from the outside and through authors who treated them as "a disease."[36]

Unlike Freud and his sources, Canetti claimed to "know the masses from within" from his own "experience," which allowed him to discover that the masses were not only around, but "inside" him,[37] since "there was a mass instinct in permanent conflict with the individualistic instinct, and the struggle between the two made it possible to explain the course of human history."[38] Canetti acknowledged that his discovery was perhaps nothing new, but he also insisted on its importance to his life. This discovery would have freed himself intellectually after his break with Freud, taking him meanwhile as the "adversary" and "model" in his long reflection on the masses, which finally materialized in *Crowds and Power*.[39]

Canetti: The Masses as a Space of Equality

Freud is deliberately and systematically omitted from *Crowds and Power*, but he is always there, like a lurking specter. The argument starts from a fear of proximity that can already be attributed to Freud, who is precisely characterized for Canetti by his fear, his distance, and his resistance to the masses. What Freud, Le Bon, and others feel can be summarized in *Crowds and Power* as the "fear of being touched," from which we only free ourselves when "we abandon ourselves to the crowd" and "reach this ideal situation, we are all the same," we feel others "as we feel ourselves," and "everything happens as if within

---

[34] E. Canetti, *Masa y poder* (1960), Random House Mondadori, Barcelona, 2009.

[35] E. Canetti, *Historia de una vida* (1980), Galaxia Gutenberg, Barcelona, 2003, pp. 534-535.

[36] *Ibid.*, p. 535.

[37] *Ibid.*, p. 536.

[38] *Ibid.*, p. 509.

[39] *Ibid.*, pp. 508-509.

a single body."[40] What is revealed, then, is unity and total equality, in which there seems to be no place for any leader.

The position of leadership, so fundamental for Freud, is practically absent from Canetti's reflection. What is present is power, but it does not correspond to what Freud understands through the figure of the primal father. This father, when mentioned in *Crowds and Power*, is associated with Australian Aranda myths in which the father figure Karora operates as a "mother of crowds" who "self-multiply" into throngs of larvae and humans that sprout from her body and devour it, as in Freud, but are also devoured by it in a "double and reciprocal" cannibalism that amounts to a "self-ingestion."[41] The masses and their father or mother are two faces of the same phenomenon that totally differ from Freud's horde.

What is displayed in the Karora myth is not a patriarchal structure with an all-powerful man monopolizing women but a figure as masculine as it is feminine that extends into the masses of descendants. Subsequently, there is a complex self-ingestion of this paternal—maternal figure, not a simple ingestion of the father by the children. Finally, instead of the children identifying with the father, we have an identity between the paternal—maternal figure and the masses in the self-multiplication of the first that gives rise to the second. The masses and their leader, if we can speak here of a "leader," really share the same being. Power is reciprocal, circulates, and spreads, and is not concentrated at one point.

For Canetti, the crowds proper, the "open crowds," are neutralized when they are "domesticated" to subdue them and to impose "obedience" on them, thus converting them into the religious and military "closed crowds" on which Freud significantly concentrated.[42] This differentiation between open and closed crowds somehow reissues the Hobbesian distinction between the multitude, which is open by definition, and the people, which already implies a certain closure that is constitutive of groups for Freud.

Unlike the Freudian closed-popular masses, the Canettian open-multitudinous ones are characterized by their "absolute and

---

[40] E. Canetti, *Masa y poder, op. cit.*, p. 70.
[41] *Ibid.*, pp. 501-515.
[42] *Ibid.*

indisputable equality" that "possesses such fundamental importance that one could almost define the state of the crowds as a state of absolute equality."[43] Canetti even affirms that "all egalitarian theories draw their energy, ultimately, from the experience of equality that each one knows in his/her own way from the crowds."[44] It is as if participation in the crowds were the material base that would allow each subject to conceive of equality.

Canetti's reasoning completes his questioning of Freudian theory: If Freud did not reflect in egalitarian terms and believed he discovered a horde in any social phenomenon, it was because he was never part of the open crowds. That is, Freud never experienced the egalitarian core of social life, the fraternal factor irreducible to the paternal one and, therefore, could not contemplate it, either. Let us say, in Marxist and Luxemburgian terms, that Freudian theory ideologically misinterpreted equality as an expression of envy and rivalry because it thought through the ideology with which the patriarchal bourgeois society of its time was justified instead of thinking through the practice of the masses, which is a fundamental moment of theory understood in a materialist sense.

What we learn from Canetti is that only through the practice of the masses is it possible to surpass individualistic ideological representations, dominant in psychoanalysis and especially in psychology, in which social phenomena are explained by the selfish interest of oedipal, possessive, and competitive individuals who would rival and envy each other. Of course, this explanation, which reduces society to market logic, is adequate and effective for elucidating the most diverse aspects of individual and social existence in a capitalist environment. However, when analyzing phenomena such as the communist movement studied by Federn, we need the direct experience of the masses, the *living school of events* that Luxemburg, herself, opposed to *schoolteachers*.

Reich and Canetti Before the 1927 Vienna Revolt

With arguments similar to those of Rosa Luxemburg, Canetti revolted against Freud and considered him to lack direct knowledge of

---

[43] *Ibid.*, p. 88.
[44] *Ibid.*

the crowd to discover its egalitarian nucleus. The crowd represented by Canetti allows us to know equality by "feeling equal" and by freeing ourselves from all "distances" and "hierarchies" that separate us.[45] This freedom correlates with equality. We discover ourselves as equals when the masses free us from what divides us into inequality.

Canetti fully knew the egalitarian and libertarian aspects of crowds when he joined the thousands of socialist workers who revolted in Vienna in July 1927, burning down the Palace of Justice and suffering fierce repression by the police and the *Heimwehr*, a fascist paramilitary organization similar to the German *Freikorps*. In this revolt, in which almost ninety workers were murdered, Canetti "completely dissolved" into the crowd.[46] Thus, he was able to experience what he later judged as characteristic of open crowds, such as their spontaneity, their freedom and their equality, their lack of leadership, and their "unitary feeling."[47]

What Canetti experienced contrasts with what Wilhelm Reich felt in the same revolt of July 1927, in which he was also present, being equally moved by what he witnessed. Although Reich apparently kept a certain distance and did not dissolve into the crowd, the revolt made him join the Communist Party, start reading Marx, and build between 1927 and 1934 the most elaborate Freudo-Marxist system of the time. Perhaps all this was in some way driven by the crowd that flooded Vienna in 1927 because, as Reich noted when narrating that revolt, "when a crowd runs, one feels an irresistible urge to run with it."[48] The Reichian way of running with it was a political-sexual activism against much of what materialized in the Vienna Palace of Justice that was burned down in 1927.

Like Canetti, Reich was drawn in and swept along by the crowd, but his disposition seemed less aesthetic, less passionate, and more intellectual. Reich recognized that the events of 1927 responded to "a genuine reaching out for justice,"[49] but he did not fail to note that, far from being a class struggle of the workers against the capitalists, it was

---

[45] *Ibid.*, pp. 73-74.
[46] E. Canetti, *Historia de una vida, op. cit.*, p. 638.
[47] *Ibid.*, pp. 638-645.
[48] W. Reich, *People in Trouble* (1953), Farrar, Straus and Giroux, New York, 1976, p. 25.
[49] *Ibid.*, p. 32.

a battle of the "people warring here with their own kind."[50] This was how Reich discovered the "irrationalism of politics" to which he would dedicate many reflections in the following years.[51]

Family Foundation of the Closed Masses

Notably, Reich located the irrationality of the 1927 revolt not in the protesters but in the policemen who fired at them. As Reich will explain later, behaviors like those of these policemen, or workers who do not rebel against their exploitation, constitute expressions of "irrationality" that must be elucidated by psychology; meanwhile, popular insurrections, just like the strikes of the exploited or the robberies committed by miserable people, are perfectly "rational" acts.[52] These acts respond rationally to socioeconomic factors and do not require psychological elucidation in terms of drives, rumors, suggestions, prejudice, stereotypes, unconscious complexes, and other "irrational motives" such as those used by the "reactionary psychology" to discredit revolutionary movements.[53]

When Reich criticized reactionary psychology, he was not thinking of the Freudian theory of groups, since Freud never addressed his metapsychological concepts to the rebellious masses. It is revealing that the two groups with which Freud exemplified his theory were the military and the ecclesiastical-religious, which, in fact, do not even correspond to the collective entities that we think of when we speak of crowds and masses. For Canetti, this detail compromised Freud's vision, but we can see it as the key point by which this vision can be saved and legitimized from a radical critical perspective.

Unlike mass psychologies like Le Bon's, Freud's is not applied to multitudes, to open crowds like the one that burned down the Palace of Justice in Vienna, but rather to closed crowds like the Church, which immediately condemned the 1927 uprising, or the Army, the model of the policemen and paramilitaries that fired on the rebels. These closed crowds are crossed by power and united by identification, comparable to the Hobbesian people configured as hordes and

---

[50] *Ibid.*, p. 24.
[51] *Ibid.*
[52] W. Reich, *The Mass Psychology of Fascism* (1933), Orgone, New York, 1946, p. 15.
[53] *Ibid.*

directed by leaders in whom the primal father is reincarnated. It is also the closed crowds that act irrationally for Reich, who showed great acuity when applying Freudian social concepts to murderous policemen, not to their victims.

Recalling the 1927 massacre, Reich approved Freud's ideas, as the primal horde "came into play" through policemen who acted like sons by "submitting to the all-powerful father" in a "servile identification with the leader."[54] Hence, the Freudian hypothesis was accepted for the police group. Reich's only objection was that Freud "eternalized the facts" by anchoring them in a certain representation of the family, a matrix of the horde, perceived as a "biological institution."[55] It is here that Reich touches the heart of the matter.

How can we not agree with Reich when he questions the supposedly ahistorical, natural, and universal character of Freudian groups? Freud seems to have been misguided in believing that humans would be condemned at all times and in all places to form groups like the people in Hobbes or like the Church, the Army, or the squads of policemen who shot at the protesters in 1927. The mistake, then, would be to assume that men were horde animals in general by their very nature.

Freud erred in naturalizing the cultural-historical institution of the bourgeois nuclear family with its Oedipal structure projected onto the primordial horde. This structure, which the Viennese rebels partly challenged in 1927, does not even seem to exist in certain cultures that escaped Western colonization. Not all humans are the horde animals that Freud envisions.

As Malinowski already noted in the same year of 1927, the Oedipus Complex corresponds to a modern European family founded on "patrilineal descent," sustained by "Roman law and Christian morality," and determined by "the economic conditions" of the bourgeoisie.[56] It is the patriarchal ideology of this bourgeoisie that imposes the particular forms of individuality, masculinity, possessiveness, rivalry, and competitiveness revealed in the Oedipal drama and its prehistor-

---

[54] W. Reich, *People in Trouble, op. cit.*, p. 28.

[55] *Ibid.*

[56] B. Malinowski, *La sexualité et sa répression dans les sociétés primitives* (1927), Payot, Paris, 1976, p. 16.

ic staging in the primal horde. The prehistory imagined by Freud is nothing more than a bourgeois drama of love, power, jealousy, and revenge.

There are good reasons to question the invalid universalization of the cultural-historical perspective underlying Freudian social theory. However, this theory hits on something crucial that became the core of the Reichian psychology of the masses. Reich owes Freud the understanding of the family foundation of that particular group configuration that Hobbes first found in the people, Freud later detected in the Church and in the Army, and Reich finally recognized in the Fascist movements of the interwar period.

Filial-Patriarchal and Fraternal-Matriarchal Structures

According to Reich's compelling hypothesis, Nazi fascism is based on a particular version of the patriarchal, authoritarian, and repressive family. This culturally and historically determined family is, as Reich puts it, the "factory" in which the "structure and ideology" of the ultra-right authoritarianism of the first half of the 20th century are produced.[57] The very subjects who follow Mussolini, Hitler, and Franco, the subjects who oppress as much as they allow themselves to be oppressed, are "patriarchal men" engendered by the "patriarchal authoritarian sexual order" that operates primarily through the family.[58] Patriarchy is a fundamental ingredient of the Nazi and Fascist masses, which can be understood through the Freudian representation of the all-powerful father of the primordial horde.

As Reich illustrates, Freud can help us study certain mass phenomena, from the Church and the Army to Nazi-Fascism and the new far-right populisms that clearly obey patriarchal logic. This logic, however, is not the only one that determines mass phenomena. There is another logic that we can conceive of as real or potentially existing on the horizon or on the edges, in a marginal or subterranean place, repressed or forgotten.

---

[57] W. Reich, *The Mass Psychology of Fascism, op. cit.*, pp. 24-25.
[58] *Ibid.*, p. 74.

Espousing the vision of prehistory that goes from Bachofen[59] and Morgan[60] to Marx[61] and Engels,[62] Reich believes that the repressive and hierarchical patriarchy was preceded by a freer and more egalitarian matriarchy. The transition from the matriarchal multitude to patriarchal people happens in the Reichian perspective "by depriving women, children, and adolescents of sexual freedom, by making a commodity out of sexuality, and by putting sexuality in the service of economic servitude."[63] In Reich, as in Marx and Engels, the patriarchy is inseparable from a class society. Correspondingly, it is inseparable from the capitalist exploitation of modern society.

Patriarchy intervenes by itself, as well as through classism and capitalism, in the constitutive equation of modern masses-hordes, such as the religious, the military, and Nazi-Fascists or neo-Nazis and neo-Fascists. These masses-hordes have a pyramidal structure and obey a filial-patriarchal logic in which there are only two kinds of figures: the paternal ones of the leaders and those of their followers, who behave like their children. As for the other masses, such as the communists accompanied by Luxemburg, they seem to obey a logic in which, as Federn already observed, the subjects opt for "fraternity," reject the "organizational pyramid that provides the ideal framework for the relationship between the father and the son," and "no longer want to be neither one nor the other." For Federn, these masses have their "psychological system" in the "fraternal relationship" and reconfigure the family order "according to the matriarchy."[64]

There are, then, masses with a fraternal-matriarchal structure in which the primordial horde that Freud conjectured does not resurrect. These masses demonstrate the crisis of patriarchy to which Durkheim, Lacan, and Federn referred. They correspond neither to the Freudian psychology of the masses nor to the Reichian social psychology of Fascism. They are free and egalitarian masses that subvert the repressive authoritarian family criticized in Reich. They are open crowds like

---

[59] J. Jakob Bachofen, *Myth, Religion, and Mother Right* (1861), Princeton University Press, New York, 1992.

[60] L. Morgan, *Ancient Society* (1877), Harvard University Press, New York, 2019.

[61] K. Marx, *The Ethnological Notebooks* (1882), Van Gorcum, Assen, 1974.

[62] F. Engels, *The Origin of the Family, Private Property and the State* (1884), International, New York, 1972.

[63] W. Reich, *The Mass Psychology of Fascism, op. cit.*, p. 74.

[64] *Ibid.*, pp. 163-164.

those to whom Canetti gave himself up in Berlin in 1922 and Vienna in 1927. According to the Hobbesian distinction, these masses cannot be reduced to the condition of the people. They are realizations of the multitudinous *potentia* on which Spinoza's politics bets.

Two kinds of Masses, Two Origins and Foundations, and Two Psychologies

The great question is whether the multitudes to which we have just referred have a place in the Freudian theoretical system. If this system locates the origin of the filial-patriarchal masses in the primal horde, where do the fraternal-matriarchal multitudes originate, and where are they founded? Freud gives us the answer in *Totem and Taboo*, when he conjectures a first social organization established after the murder of the primal father, founded on the homosexual "feelings and acts" of the brothers expelled from the horde, configured by the "institution of matriarchy," and "replaced by the patriarchal organization."[65] Many years later, in *Moses and Monotheism*, Freud still recognized the transition by which "the matriarchal structure of society was replaced by a patriarchal one."[66]

Freud can universalize patriarchy because it has reigned in human civilization since the most remote times. However, it is now in a crisis that dates to the 19th century, which is expressed in psychoanalysis, and which has been the flag not only of feminism and the sexual revolution, but also of revolutionary masses such as those that rocked Europe between 1917 and 1919. Analyzing retrospectively that convulsed period, we are in a position to conjecture that the *Freikorps* that launched against those movements in Berlin and that assassinated Rosa Luxemburg constituted reactions against the same crisis of patriarchy. We found the same reactions in the Austrian *Heimwehr* and in the other Nazi-Fascist paramilitary organizations of the interwar period. All these organizations and their far-right descendants in later decades can be considered reactionary precisely because they react against the crisis of the old patriarchal order and fight to preserve it.

The difference between reactionary and progressive masses is more structural than it first appears. The first ones, in which the pri-

---

[65] S. Freud, *Totem and Taboo, op. cit.*, p. 167.
[66] S. Freud, *Moses and Monotheism*, The Hogarth Press, Letchworth, 1939, p. 180.

mal horde is resurrected, are dominated by the "individual psycholo-gy" that Freud attributes to the "father, chief, or leader," while the later ones seem to obey what appears as "social psychology" in the Freud-ian vision: the psychology of sons who "advanced from identification with one another to homosexual object-love."[67] This progress can be associated with the revolutionary orientation of the fraternal-matriar-chal masses, which opposes them to the reactionary orientation of the filial-patriarchal masses.

The opposition between the two kinds of masses is also an opposition between revolution and reaction, and progressivism and conservatism. It is also a contradiction between social and individual psychology, between socialism and bourgeois individualism, between communism and egoism, and between sexuality and narcissism, a con-tradiction that we have already analyzed in previous works.[68] As we have also tried to demonstrate elsewhere, all this can be read in Freud, but on the condition of reading him *symptomally*, reading him as he taught us to listen, paying attention to the symptoms of the word.[69]

---

[67] S. Freud, *Group Psychology and the Analysis of the Ego, op. cit.*, pp. 122-123.

[68] D. Pavón-Cuéllar, "El violento salto del narcisismo al socialismo," in Orozco Guz-mán, M. and Soria Escalante, H. (eds.), *Narcisismo infame: reflexiones psicoanalíticas*, UMSNH y Porrúa, Mexico City, 2016. See also: "Narcisismo, ideología y psicología," in América Espinosa, Adalberto Levi Hambra and Juan Capetillo (eds.), *A cien años de "In-troducción del narcisismo,"* Universidad Veracruzana Xalapa, 2014.

[69] D. Pavón-Cuéllar, "Another Freud for the Left: Our Group Psychology and the Analy-sis of Ourselves," *Psychotherapy and Politics International*, 19(3), 2001. See also: "Hacia otra psicología freudiana de las masas: más allá del gran crustáceo y su loca invertebra-da," *Desde el jardín de Freud: revista de psicoanálisis* 21, pp. 179-198.

The Lessons of an Absent Teacher: Freud's *Massenpsychologie und Ich-analyse*, and the Losses of White Melancholia in South Africa and the United States

Rosalind C. Morris

> "...riot defendants [...] have claimed their presence in the building was a result of being "caught up" in the hysteria of the crowd."[1]

> "The Jan. 6 assault on the Capitol by a violent mob at the behest of former president Donald Trump was an act of political violence intended to alter the outcome of a legitimate democratic election. [...] the insurrection was the result of a large, diffuse and new kind of protest movement congealing in the United States. [...] Those involved are [...] 95 percent White and 85 percent male."[2]

Everywhere, groups of white supremacists are on the move. Media platforms are aflame with incendiary myth, which travels like a spark to connect dispersed and anonymous viewers. In the streets and on the digital screen, masses circulate as fearful specters and lures. Watching, some feel themselves captive to a nightmare they thought they had seen before, and which surprises them because they believed they had left this horror behind. But no. Windows break. There is the sound of booted feet marching. When courts release their verdicts on the extrajudicial killing of Black men and women, white supremacists, anti-racist activists, and prudent pragmatists alike stock their cup-

---

[1] "Rioters claim crowd at the Jan 6 Insurrection was to blame," *Tampa Bay Times*, May 21, 2021, https://www.tampabay.com/news/nation-world/2021/05/23/rioters-claim-the-crowd-at-the-jan-6-capitol-insurrection-was-to-blame/.

[2] R. A. Pape, "What an analysis of 377 Americans arrested or charged in the Capitol insurrection tells us," *The Washington Post*, April 6, 2021, https://www.washingtonpost.com/opinions/2021/04/06/capitol-insurrection-arrests-cpost-analysis/.

boards in anticipation of confrontations between what they assume will be the crowds of discontent.

Ours is a crowded time. A time crowded by images of crowds—crowds being groups of people who, Freud tells us, think in images.[3] Always ambiguous, at once the figure of revolutionary possibility and counterrevolutionary vengefulness, the crowd and the mass today are the most overt forms of appearance of an apparently resurgent and regressive politics of group identity, especially among white suprem-acists. Sometimes glossed as populism and sometimes condemned as fascism, the rise and global consolidation of white supremacist and na-tionalist populism during the past decade has generated a broad con-sensus among analysts. At its heart, they observe, is the sense of loss and displacement suffered by groups that had presumed their right to dominance. That they did not always enjoy such dominance has little bearing on this sensation of loss. Indeed, these groups are hetero-geneous in socioeconomic terms. What binds them is neither shared experience nor a shared location in the politico-economic field. It is, rather, an affect (or complex of affects) substituting for an identity. Ac-cordingly, putatively shared racial identity may be supplanted by one of national and/or ideological affiliation without threatening group co-hesion (as when, in the United States, conservative members of racial minorities join white supremacists in ostensible defense of national integrity). And their representatives acknowledge their own internal difference when they enunciate their rationale as a right to recover that group coherence that they discern in minority formations. That is, their own coalescence is haunted by a kind of mimetic desire to be in the place of those whom they believe have usurped their place.

There is a certain satisfaction to be had in this brief descrip-tion. But ultimately, it discloses little more than what is projected on the digital screens of late-/post-/anti-modern myth: a zombified world wherein the antiquated aspiration to eternity gives itself over to the mob-figures of living death. Our need at present is not merely to reit-erate the descriptions of phenomena. It is to analyze and understand this situation in a manner that permits its transformation.

The one hundredth anniversary of Freud's essay occasions an uncanny sensation of familiarity. It seems to have awaited recent

---

[3] S. Freud, *Massenpsychologie und Ich-Analyse*, Gesammelte Werke XIII, S. Fischer Verlag, Frankfurt, 1987, p. 78. All subsequent citations will be in parentheses.

events to reveal its prophetic truth. But its more relevant and challenging attribute lies in what it can teach us about the resonances between the affect that characterizes both the ressentiment-driven populists oriented by white supremacy *and* its melancholic critics. Doing so requires that we interrogate precisely this sense of the familiar and all that codes resemblance and relation, as well as identity, in the idiom of genealogical descent. It requires a questioning of every recourse to the metaphorics of a social logic, from the secret society to the state, that goes by the name of 'family.' This notion of the family is perhaps the most potent concept-metaphor of the genetic and generic basis of identity in the apparent resurgence of the phenomena described by Freud. Certainly, others have attempted to read populism and especially fascism as a function of the sexual pressures and psychodynamics of patriarchalized and especially Oedipalized family structures.[4] However, my purpose here is different. It is a call for a historicization of the resemblance. This does not imply a choice between continuity and rupture-repetition but a need to understand what happened in a long century of radical transformations in every sphere of life—differently but no less thoroughly in every part of the world—such that differences arising in time could appear *as* continuity.

I propose that what appeared in dominant discourse as the *apparent endings* of white supremacy in the two countries that were popularly considered to be its most hospitable loci, namely South Africa and the United States, encouraged its diffusion and reappearance on a global scale. The fall of Apartheid in South Africa and the election of Barack Obama in the US were coded in dominant liberal and left-leaning discourse as watershed moments in the struggle to overcome racism. But they were also coded as watershed moments in white supremacist discourse—as losses of legitimate, historically earned authority. On both sides, of hoped-for-gain and felt loss, this misrecognition allowed a formal achievement to stand for an actual transformation, with the result being complacency on one side and a regressive defense of white group identity on the other. But this is only part of the story. The other part of the story has to do with the incapacity of many critics to fully analyze the affects, and especially the

---

[4] For example: W. Reich, *Die Massenpsychologie des Faschismus* (1933), and Gilles Deleuze and Felix Guattari's *Capitalisme et schizophrénie. L'anti-Œdipe* (1972).

melancholia, that they share with the white supremacists whom they otherwise repudiate.

To make this argument, I will undertake three distinct movements. Beginning with a rereading of Freud's essay, I hope to draw out what I believe are the still-persuasive elements of his analysis, while interrogating the gendered axiomatics subtending it and paying particular attention to the place of analogy in both the reading practice that he develops in the essay, and in the pathogenesis that he is attempting to elucidate. I read Freud's essay as both a symptomatic description and attempted analysis of his historical moment, but also as a narrative of the mythopoetic and empirical-historical processes by which political communities (the good groups of his essay) come into being through the substitution of fraternity and the leader-function for siblingship and the maternal function. Such a development, I intend to argue, was irreducibly tied to the production of race during the century that preceded Freud's writing and this has only been intensified in the century that the centenary of his essay concludes. This is one reason why the threat of the mass, the mob, and the panicked leaderless group of Freud's time and our own is addressed with such passional vociferousness by white supremacists. Freud was unable to think this development as an effect of racialization on a global scale, nor to theorize the relationship between antisemitism and antiBlack racism. Yet because of the simultaneous resemblance between what he describes and what we see, and because of his theory's constitutive blindnesses, we will be helped by rereading Freud.

My aim is to both affirm and bring to crisis his analysis in a deconstructionist mode, while reflecting on the world to which it refers. This requires some distance—and some political economy. Believing that the understanding of what is most immediate is best generated through a comparativist gesture, I will therefore move from Freud's essay to sketch out some of the elements of white supremacist discourse in its relationship to group formation in South Africa in the moment of his writing, against the backdrop of the globalization of what Du Bois called the "Colour Line" in the aftermath of World War I (but bearing in mind the resemblance *and difference* between the racial formation that developed in the United States and in South Africa). My purpose for selecting South Africa is not only because it is the object and site of my research, but because its function as metonym and misrecognized locus of white supremacy and segregationism in the post-World War II period, under the signature of "Apartheid," is linked to the resurgence of which I shall speak. My aims in this section of the essay will therefore be to track the movement of Freud's thought, as he leaves the analysis of war neuroses for more general questions of massification, and to consider its reception in South Africa by white conservative and liberal writers, who were then the object of critique by Black writers of both liberal and radical tendencies. The comparison must take account of the differences between white supremacism in a society (the US) whose minority Black population was largely descendent of slaves, and one where the majority Black population was mainly descendent of free but colonized people. But in both, the disavowal of Black fraternity was linked to a violent displacement of Black maternity *in the interests of white property.* Fear of the loss of this property informed white supremacism in both cases, but Freud has taught us to understand this concern as having a dimension not only of property but of the "proper" or propriety of social identity. Accordingly, in both cases, we are led to repose the question of the family and the group that so preoccupied Freud as both psychosocial formations *and as* economic institutions grounded in the contractualist axiomatics of liberal capitalism.

No doubt this risks wrenching Freud 'out of context.' But is this not required in every moment when we want to learn from a text, rather than merely assign it to the status of archival evidence of that which has been surpassed? Thus, historicizing and dehistoricizing, simultaneously contextualizing and decontextualizing *Massenpsychologie und Ich-Analyse,* will now turn and return to Freud's essay in an effort to recover what might otherwise be lost. Loss is, indeed, the kernel of this story.

The Losses of Group Psychology and the Analysis of the Ego

Group Psychology and the Analysis of the Ego [Massenpsychologie und Ich-Analyse] is in many respects a text of loss, perhaps even a text that was on the verge of being lost to social theory, before the 'insurrection' of January 6, 2021, made it appear both newly salient and retrospectively prescient. Loss punctuates its discourse, animates its theorizing, and operates the critical comparativism that permits Freud to both recapitulate and distance himself from the argument put forth in Gustave Le Bon's *Psychologie des Foules* (1895). In contradistinction to Le Bon's otherwise often persuasive account, Freud proposes a taxonomy of groups [*Massen*] oriented not by the mere fact of number or the transience of their existence, but by the distinction between formations with and without leaders. Heretofore, the leaderless group had been understood primarily as a mob of potentially violent tendencies, in which the psyches of individuals were distorted by being submerged in a mass. In these readings, the magnitude of the mass was itself an explanation for individuals' loss of self-control and autonomy. It was also associated with the mob of lower class, antiauthoritarian and revolutionary tendencies. Indeed, a barely secreted conjoining of the *Masse/foule*/group with the Terror haunts much of the nineteenth century discourse on the phenomenon. Until Freud. Freud's work marks a transition from the thinking of the mass as exception to a recognition of its generalized status in modernity.[5] But the leaderless group is not merely a group without a leader in Freud's account; it is a social formation in which the dramaturgy of the primal father's impatient and jealous execution by his sons recurs as a structural and thus de-temporalized phenomenon. Hence, for him, the question of the group and of massification is always also a question of the leader, whose presence permits stabilization in the absence of more perduring institutional forms. One might read Freud's intervention, then, as a corollary of the transition from the theoretical and perhaps historical-empirical linkage between the mass and antiauthoritarianism, on one hand, and populism and authoritarianism on the other. But this is to get ahead of our story.

Beyond the doubled loss of a patriarch and of time, of patriarchal timing, there are many other losses in Freud's essay. There is the loss of the inhibitions that the individual exhibits when in a group. There is the loss of the love-object, whose lamentation and subsequent introjection marks the melancholic—a figure who will provide Freud with the paradigm for thinking the dynamics between the group and its leader. The loss of the leader in the durable group, and especially the army, is also granted significance when seen as a source of panic, which phenomenon prompts Freud's questions about the libid-

---

[5] S. Jonsson, "After Individuality: Freud's Mass Psychology and Weimar Society," *New German Critique* 119, 2013, pp. 53-75, p. 55.

inal ties said to enable and define the group. In the army, he says, such panic leads to directionless, self-interested, and self-preserving flight. In the Church, it leads to indiscriminate murderousness. Freud even suggests that the 'natural' and 'ruthless' cruelty and hostility that religious groups show to non-believers would be directed to all neighbors in the absence of a leader, a deity or Christ-figure, in whom they would find the source of their mutual bond as equal objects of his love.[6]

Already emerging in this litany of loss is the specter of that group whom Freud counterposes to the mob, with its instinctual rapacity: a group of civilizational capacity, moral restraint, and collective accomplishment. This positive conception of the group arises only because Freud considers the group by way of analogy with the individual, arguing that the tendencies that organize and impel its operations are to be found not at the level of the large collective but in the smaller groups which are its originary kernel: "the social instinct may not be a primitive one and insusceptible of dissection, and . . . it may be possible to study the beginnings of its development in a narrower circle, such as that of the family." In brief, the individual is originarily produced and thus intelligible only within the family which, for Freud, is a nucleated patriarchal formation with a father as its structural head.

The story that Freud tells in *Massenpsychologie* (and in *Totem and Taboo*) is organized around the originary role of the father *and his displacement*. This father is reproduced in the simulacral form of the ego ideal, which generates group stability—an ambivalent development that is at once the basis of civilizational progress and the source of cruel violence. Civilization, which is to say political society, is fraternal for Freud. Fraternity is not a neutral figure for amity, lateral solidarity or political community. It is irreducibly gendered male.[7] Of course, this internal presumption has generated much critical antipathy to Freud's text. Anchored in, if not reduced to the figural narrative of

---

[6] Freud's privileging of the Christian/Pauline discourse of love in the conception of fraternal solidarity and mutual immunization from violence within all religions nonetheless begs Derrida's question, and a fuller reading would have to ask after the "Christian semantics of fraternity." See *Politics of Friendship*, trans. George Collins, Verso, New York, 1997, p. 96.

[7] The development, in Freud's own time and since, of counter-political formations under the name of sisterhood only proves this point; their derivativeness and political ineffectuality is a function of both the incapacity to permit the female to signify the universal in Western metaphysical traditions, and the exceptionalization of the female leader.

the nucleated family, Freud's analysis has sometimes been dismissed as a normativization and ontologization of the bourgeois patriarchal family form, whence he derived his observations. But such a relativist historicization may risk another loss—of the understanding of loss (and of the misrecognition of lack as loss) that could otherwise help us grasp our contemporary scene. Nor can the affects of melancholia and enraged vindictiveness driving white supremacism today be entirely disentangled from the intergenerational conflict that Freud coded as patricidal aggressivity. Rather than dismiss the myth as a mere recapitulation of ideological norms, we should inquire into the forms in which it is repeated at present. We can begin by observing that, often, the name of the father is simply, 'politics.'

In the US today, right wing discourse is often animated by intergenerational hostility. Under the sign of politics, old guards are denounced on the grounds of their corruption, self-interest, lack of knowledge of working-class (blue collar) life, or excessive submission to institutionality. Ossification and putrefaction converge in the mixed metaphor of the swamp. This linguistic breeder of monstrosity is an expression of the hatred of authority, *and the desire for it.* It is important to recognize the absence of a critique of leadership even in those spaces where apparent anti-statism or a repudiation of 'politics' is most vociferous. The old guards are reviled in conservative discourse precisely because it has found so many perfect substitutes: strongmen who offer absolute authority as consolation for the directionlessness attributed to the liberal democratic orders in which they emerge. The compensations these strongmen promise make sense only insofar as the figure of the leader is both valorized and experienced as lost.

I do not introduce this palimpsest of loss in response to the insurrection of January 6, 2021, or the years immediately preceding it, as a form of mourning. To mourn what preceded the insurrection would imply a belief that it was merely the failure to realize the liberal ideals travestied by the antiliberalism of strongmen regimes that is the core of our era's crisis (not only in the US—where it is as much parodied as realized—but in Brazil, Britain, India, Russia, Belorussia, Hungary, Poland, North Korea, Turkey, and beyond). But we cannot conflate the lost with the good. Following Freud's example from "Thoughts for the Times on War and Death" (1915) we cannot mourn what we had not achieved. Without mourning, then, we must contend with the phantasmatic force of loss as both a negation (for the right) and a success now at risk of being overturned (for the left). Let us then return to Freud's essay.

The Missing Teacher and the Lost Girls: Of Translation by Analogy

Other losses have occurred as Freud's text has passed from German into English. Take, for example, the introductory statement of the essay, wherein Freud lists the relations he deems to be social, as opposed to narcissistic: those of "an individual to his parents and to his brothers and sisters, to the object of his love, and to his physician." This is the official translation of *The Standard Edition.* The German text includes in this list, along with siblings, lovers, parents, and the physician, the "Lehrer" or teacher (*"zu seinem Lehrer und zu seinem Artz"*). Where there had been a teacher, then, there is only a mute space, unless one turns back to Freud's mother-tongue and the language in which he would be banished in the name of the Fatherland. However, the discovery of a translational discontinuity is less of error in a translator's rendition than of making the visibility of this discontinuity an incitement to reading.

What can one think when the effacement of the teacher is made visible? The absence doesn't become an image, not even the image of a gap, by being exposed. Rather, it solicits the historical imagination, which works at least partly by analogizing.[8] Hence a double session is opened. For, it is this faculty that a reading between Freud's text, *in its own time* and in the moment of its centenary, requires. However, when the scenes described in one era resemble so closely those of a distant epoch, the temptation to analogizing needs to be tempered by the recognition of those differences that would be elided by the desire to render the past as prophecy or direct commentary on the present.

Let us then attend to the unanticipated transformation of the text in translation. If, for example, the translation is read in the United States, the absenting of the teacher in the passage from German to English might be understood to *allegorize* a history of education's denigration (via a funding structure that separates private and public

---

[8] Reason is here understood as the faculty for producing syllogism, and deriving determined consequences therefrom. Analogy posits resemblances, but does not yet entail the derivation of causal dependency.

education, and that ties public education, via taxation, to the wealth of those who inhabit the territory in which its formal institutions are located). Here, the absence would be the trace of an effacement. In a certain sense, the teacher is always under threat of erasure in the American milieu.

It may be mere coincidence that the translational elision corresponds to the undervaluation of education in the society which is also the destiny of the translation. But Freud has taught us to read coincidences as ciphers for accessing the unconscious that perceives them. Education is now a veritable battleground in the so-called new culture wars, as white supremacists try to reclaim what they fear they have lost: control of the historical narrative in which their privilege and prerogative were mythified.[9] In these conflicts, white supremacists assail the possibility that Freud's text recognized, namely that teachers are figures of authority who displace parents. Hence, their roles in dispensing a counter-narrative to white supremacy are repudiated and they are accused of usurping the rights of parents in the patriarchal family. The absence of the teacher can therefore be read as a kind of wish fulfillment for the right, and a specter of social and political loss for the left. But only in the mode of *allegory*. This is crucial. For, Freud's text does not actually *refer to* the US scene; it can only teach us to *read* the US scene. This is why speculation on the *allegorical* meaning of Freud's text *for the United States* (or any other site) must lead back to an engagement with the story of pathological sociality that anchors the text itself, where the narrative of the hysterical school girls leads *not to allegory but to analogy*.

The hysterical schoolgirls provide Freud with the ur-image of the pathological mass. They have this function for the narrative structure of his essay, where they appear as the first instance of neurotic identification (following the description of the boy's normative development). Within the pseudo-historical logic of societal devel-

---

[9] The '1619 Project,' which aimed to broaden the coverage of slave and racism in American history and in school curricula, was specifically targeted by the Trump Administration, leading the Heritage Foundation to denounce Critical Race Theory as a threat to the constitutional republic. See S. Sawchuck, "What is Critical Race Theory and why is it Under Attack," *Education Week*, May 18, 2021, https://www.edweek.org/leadership/what-is-critical-race-theory-and-why-is-it-under-attack/2021/05. Also see J. Barr, "Critical Race Theory is the Hottest Topic on Fox News," *The Washington Post*, June 24, 2021, https://www.washingtonpost.com/media/2021/06/24/critical-race-theory-fox-news/.

opment, they represent pure, speechless identity, providing the image of that which must be overcome, via the leader, for social justice to emerge.

Reading the hysterical contagion among the schoolgirls who both envy and identify with their romantically entangled classmate, Freud notes that certain situations permit and even encourage analogizing to follow a pathological direction. The scene that opens this section of Freud's text is the stuff of penny novels and B-movies. Nonetheless, adjacent to the accounts of religious warfare, military collapse, mythological murder, and civilizational transcendence, the story of the school girls acquires new significance. Freud's text renders the girls' hysteria a scene of reading quite beyond the kind that writers as diverse as Foucault and Spivak have damned as presumptuous ventriloquism. The effort to provide the hysteric with a voice is also, these critics note, the substitution of the analyst's voice for the muted woman's.[10] This is not because of an immunity to such a desire on Freud's part—quite the contrary. But he is trying in this scene to show how the girls' behavior reveals the origins of patriarchal masculinity as the overcoming of femininity; it is a description of heteronormative ideology. He is not concerned with what the girls might be trying to say, but rather with what makes them incapable of saying that they envy each other, and that they want what the others have. Trying to explain how muteness is identity for the girls, and thereby implying an always already pathological dimension to female sociability, Freud turns to the question of why, in some cases, the normative silence of the girls becomes diseased. Now, this feminine envy is present for Freud in the masculine domain as a surpassed origin, until it resurfaces under certain conditions; recall that envy incites the primordi-

---

[10] Ironically, to expose psychiatry's incapacity to grasp the sexual desire of the hysteric, when he is accusing Charcot and Freud of substituting their discourse for the hysteric's "sexual pantomime," Foucault cannot himself resist ventriloquizing that same hysteric. He writes: "My impression is that this sexual bacchanal should be taken as the counter-maneuver by which the hysterics responded to the ascription of trauma: You want to find the cause of my symptoms, the cause that will enable you to pathologize them and enable you to function as a doctor; you want this trauma, well, you will get all my life, and you won't be able to avoid hearing me recount my life and, at the same time, seeing me mime my life anew and endlessly re-actualize it in my attacks!" M. Foucault, *Psychiatric Power. Lectures at the Collège de France, 1973-4*, ed. Jacques Lagrange, trans. Graham Burchell, Picador, New York, 2003, p. 322.

al patricide in Freud's mythic rendition of societal origins, and it is the transformation and management of envy, via subordination to the leader, that is for Freud the essence of the good group. What interests Freud after the catastrophe of World War I is why, in some situations, analogizing leads to civility and justice and why, in others, it leads to regression and pathological over-identification that erupts in nationalism and its transformation into war. In the latter instance, he speaks of a *pathogenic situation*. Sometimes, this situation permits an ostensible regression to femininity to appear in the guise of extreme and even sadistic masculinity. Because Freud's reading discloses the normative principles of a bourgeois, white-dominant society, there is something to learn by adducing his text just as he adduced Le Bon's and proceeding, by gloss and interpolation, to a conclusion that depends upon but departs from his own.

Once More into the Breach

Re-reading, we enter a scene of intense but prohibited desire. The girls are in a boarding school, sequestered from their parents and subject to their teachers' rule. One of the girls "has had a letter from someone with whom she is secretly in love which arouses her jealousy, and [...] she reacts to it with a fit of hysterics." The girl cannot grasp this otherwise normativized vulnerability to rejection, and somatizes her crisis. We surmise that the lover has expressed affection for someone else. No sooner has the girl or young woman (her status is liminal) collapsed in hysterics, than her classmates follow suit, succumbing to "mental infection." What is this contagion that leads the girls to somatize a psychic wound that is not their own? Freud explains that "the mechanism is that of identification based upon the possibility or *desire of putting oneself in the same situation*. The other girls would like to have a secret love affair too, and under the influence of a sense of guilt they also accept the suffering involved in it" (107, emphasis added). He continues against what he presumes would be the conclusion of most analysis: "It would be wrong to suppose that they take on the symptom out of sympathy. On the contrary, the sympathy only arises out of the identification, and this is proved by the fact that infection or imitation of this kind takes place in circumstances where even less pre-existing sympathy is to be assumed than usually exists between friends in a girls' school." Identification *precedes* sympathy and is its condition of possibility—this is a crucial structural as well as logical principle for Freud's analysis.

Freud assumes that the one girl's love, pursued despite the taboos upon it, could only be envied by the others. Proprietary tendencies are fundamental aspects of the psyche in Freud's psychoanalysis—and in this respect the psyche described is the always already property-desiring subject of capitalism. Yet it is less the presumptive competition and proprietariness among the girls—which, if it exists, at least requires an explanation—than the gesture it provokes that demands our attention: *"One ego has perceived a significant analogy with another upon one point* —in our example upon openness to a similar emotion; an identification is thereupon constructed on this point, and, *under the influence of the pathogenic situation*, is displaced on to the symptom which the one ego has produced. *The identification by means of the symptom* has thus become the mark of a *point of coincidence* between the two egos which has to be kept repressed" (107, emphasis added).[11]

The discovery of a shared attribute born of mutual inspection and comparison has led to an analogy, but the trajectory of the analogy and its social effect is determined not by the subject's desire but by the psychosocial situation. This situation lets the girl see in her classmates something that she recognizes as an element of herself. For this perception to generate a mass phenomenon, all the girls must be in the same or an analogous situation. It depends therefore on the homogeneity of the institutional context. A girl's boarding school is, in this sense, like an army or a church. It is serially organized by age and learning cohort. Such normative institutions do not always generate hysteria, of course. Something has to happen for the general resem-

---

[11] From his earliest writings on the subject, Freud maintains that the hysteric is subject to a transposition of affect, but unlike other phobias or neuroses, this takes a fully somatic form, and is compartmentalized so that it remains inaccessible to consciousness. See, for example, "The Neuro-Psychoses of Defence," *SE III (1893-1899): Early Psycho-Analytic Publications*, p. 41-61. Nonetheless, the idiom in which he posed the difference developed significantly. In the 1890s, Freud was thinking of the somaticization of hysteria in the idiom of and by analogy with demonic possession and witchcraft, and transposition arises as a phenomenon of belief. By 1909, however, Freud was thinking of obsessional neurosis as a "dialect" of the language of hysteria, lacking only that "leap from a mental process to a somatic innervation," also known as "hysterical conversion." That is to say, hysteria is a language that abandons language, a pathology in the linguisticality of the subject. See "Notes Upon a Case of Obsessional Neurosis," *SE X (1909)*: pp. 151-318, esp. 157.

blance to get cathected in this destructive manner. In this scene, the comparative gesture that animates the analogy and thus the identification is singular. It is "but one point." There is no mutual typification, no discernment in the other of a kind of person, with a multiplicity of attributes and generalizable traits. To the contrary, it is the discreet signifier visible above all else and that might be generic in the person, that orients the identificatory gesture. The girls will be reduced to and by that one symptom, such that their other qualities vanish. For this reason they can be ciphers for the racial group, in which the social has been reduced to a single dimension and desocialized: turned inward in narcissistic avoidance of any relation with others.

In the school that resembles a church and an army, the teacher, whose importance was indicated in the earliest part of the essay, is absented by the love object, and his withdrawal thus creates a crisis—the crisis of a twofold displacement along the axis of parent-teacher-lover.[12] Despite this compounding force and source of potential loss, Freud says the girls share a vulnerability to a single emotion born of non-recognition. The grief of loss, and more importantly of being given up. It is the emotion of all the little social deaths that demand the recurrent funeral orations of adolescent poetry. Yet, all the girls experience a social death in this instance, and not just one. Why?

The boarding school has over-valorized the teacher, inserting him (or her) into the place of the parent who is the bearer of law, the source of recognition and the threatened site of rejection that has become all the more destructive by being cathected along the analogizing series. Under these circumstances, when the teacher is replaced by the lover, and then withdraws, a crisis ensues. And massification shows itself to be a poor substitute for actual social relations of mutual dependency and entanglement. Only collapse into pathological identity seems to follow. In other words, a society organized on the principles of massification promotes or enables a misrecognition of

---

[12] The modernity of the school consists not only in the serial organization of students or the structuring of their relations by age and their subjection to disciplinary procedures that cultivate their moral as well as their corporeal attitude. It also overturns the valorization of the teacher-lover in the classical model of boys' education that defined pedagogy in Greece. We may read this modernization not as the legacy of a merged Greco-Christian tradition but rather as the imperial Romano-Germanization of that tradition. The result is the separation of the objects of desire and identification which were previously consolidated in a single figure.

social relatedness and *dependency on others becomes identity with them*. What is the relationship between this pathological identification and that other kind of identification that binds people in communities of shared inheritance, solidarity, and mutual care? How is this difference related to that other structural principle on which Freud leans so heavily, namely the difference between leader-led and leaderless groups? Anticipating our argument, we will observe that the hysterical schoolgirls will become populist masses when siblingship is replaced with fraternity.

A Leading Question: On Ressentiment and the Loss of Leadership

What is especially analytically challenging about the events of January 6 from the perspective of Freud's account is their simultaneous exhibition of the features of leaderlessness (transience, lack of a coherent idea, amoebic mobility rather than unidirectional motion) and their display of an absolute submission to the idea of the leader—in the form of Donald J. Trump (whose presence and then absence among the insurrectionists provides the temporized and dramaturgical counterpart of the structural principle).

Freud argues that the schoolgirls descend into hysteria because they cannot identify with something outside of their group, which perhaps implies that the foreclosed figure of a female leader might have saved them. However, having adduced their story in the service of analogy, Freud then casts it into the abyss of society's evolutionary prehistory—not in the manner of the primal father, whose spectral presence continues to be determining, but as a pure instance of pathology. However, what Freud unwittingly shows us is that the leader was a false solution to the deeper need which is a refusal of the mastering one, and an end to melancholia.

Melancholia is an affective state and not a political idea. Nonetheless, for Freud, there is a relationship between melancholia and ressentiment, and between ressentiment and social justice, for it is in the generalization and sublimation of ressentiment, via the leader, that he believes social justice is generated. Here, melancholia implies stasis and justice implies equality; it is the redemption of massification, rationalization, the value form in its ethically enabling translation (no equality without equivalence). However, it is also in the conjoining of melancholia and ressentiment—two negative intensities—that white supremacy and nationalist populism get their impulsive force.

Moving from the analysis of girls to the myth of the primal horde, Freud also moves from hysteria to the proper identificatory relations among children who, initially envious of each other, relinquish their mutual hatred and hostility rather than risk the opprobrium of a parent and their own more radical exile from favor: "So there grows up in the troop of children a communal or group feeling, which is then further developed *at school*. The first demand made by this reaction-formation is for justice, for equal treatment for all." This value, equality, is itself "put forward at school. If one cannot be the favourite oneself, at all events nobody else shall be the favourite." What is thus an anti-social force is metamorphosed into a social good, and Freud states that the "transformation—the replacing of jealousy by a group feeling in the nursery and classroom—might be considered improbable, if the same process could not later on be observed again in other circumstances." Once again, the example is that of "women and girls," whose adoration of a pop star, "a singer or pianist" might lead to competition but, instead, allows them to join in solidary appreciation of their shared love-object.

The girls' capacity to forge such bonds by renouncing their particular and exclusive claims is achieved without any external intervention or without submission to the teacher's rule, but it ends in pathological identity (the teacher, it turns out, was missing in the German original as well as the English translation, but in different ways— the German one unmentioned, the English one unthought). For the boys and men in the mythic tale of the originary murder of the father, something else must occur. Here, Freud transposes the structural question of sexual difference onto a historical narrative of civilizational progress. "What appears *later on* in society," he writes, namely the development of *esprit de corps* (he uses German, English, and French phrasing), also has its origins in envy. But the historical development that occurs among brothers, rather than sisters, is a notion of social justice, a form of equality achieved through self-abnegation. "Social justice means that *we deny ourselves many things so that others may have to do without them* as well, or what is the same thing, may not be able to ask for them" (120, emphasis added). Freud does not say that justice consists in the sacrifice of some things so that others may have them, or equal access to objects or rights, or a commitment to human dignity. He describes a self-deprivation whose only purpose is to ensure that *no one else has something that the subject lacks*. Justice is a bond of mutual deprivation. This transformation of spite into a principle of equality is enabled, says Freud, by an affectionate bond with someone outside of the group, and this observation leads him to describe the evolution by which the primal horde is both supplanted and remembered in the modern mass. This development runs parallel to the evolution of the leader from the original persecutorial *pater familias*, who is both supplanted and remembered in the leader as one who either loves or hates his subordinates equally, and who, by doing so, provokes their solidarity by relieving them of the suspicion that anyone is more loved (or despised) than anyone else. But the achievement remains within the genealogy of the familial, and in the mode of fraternity.

Freud adds, "Do not let us forget, however, that the demand for equality in a group applies only to its members and not to the leader." The "contrivance" by which the members of the mass bond in religious and military communities is that which misrecognizes the persecutorial and hateful relation of the leader to his subjects as one of love. Whereas the transformation of envy and ressentiment into social bonds enables the development of a political idea, that between hate and love enables the emergence only of an inverted affect. The latter sustains the former, but they are not identical.

Here, the English translation of *Massen* as groups is a liability, for the concept of the group in English admits internal stratification, whereas Freud is primarily interested in those principles that tend to the loss of such hierarchy. Significantly, the lack of differentiation is not a sociological fact; it is a function of its being perceived from without. The groups characterized by this exemplary transformation, namely the church and the military, are not spontaneously emergent, formless masses. Rather, individuals within these groups are said to exhibit the negative characteristics of massification when the leader absconds. It is *only insofar as they anticipate being perceived from without, by an other, and treated as equals in this respect*, as members of the military rather than as ranked soldiers, or as members of a single religious community rather than as laypeople, bishops, canons, cardinals, deacons, and so forth, that they are subject to that positive transformation which Freud wants to secure against the collapse to which it remains permanently vulnerable. The group can never be the scene of justice if it is entirely self-enclosed. And this, above all, is what the group must repress in order to sustain its fantasized autonomy, its hollow simulation of sovereignty. It needs an outside.

What enables the leader to become the source of identification and not just submission, says Freud, is the fact that the "individual gives up his ego ideal and substitutes for it the group ideal as embodied in the leader." He then remarks that the leader need not be a "prodigy," but only possess a relative share of the attributes that society has deemed ideal. Lacking but desiring the qualities that they have conferred upon the leader, group members identify with him and rejoice in the sensation of sharing in that which they could not claim on their own merits—even if it has been incarnated in a mediocre form. And what is this ego ideal? Freud says that it is the *"sum of all the limitations* in which the ego has had to acquiesce." By this he means all that has mitigated the sovereignty of the infant, all that is lost in the moment of being birthed, then inducted into social life. Hence, remarks Freud, the thrilled saturnalias and carnivals of transgression when the ego ideal can be 'abrogated.' And the debauchery of the mass when its leader withdraws or is withdrawn. The insurrection of January 6 showed us that the desolation and pathos of that debauchery is proportionate to the mediocrity of the leader.

Back to the Future: The Displacement of the One and the Illusion of the Two

If Freud's essay seems to provide an uncanny description of the events of January 6, it is partly because the dramaturgy of that event staged and mobilized the cohering presence and liberating (or debauching) withdrawal of the leader. But the group is already an uncanny formation in Freud's analysis, having been erected on the repression of the memory of the primal horde and the formative patricide of myth. This postulation of uncanniness is arrived at by analogy between the hypnotist and the group leader, and Freud states that the hypnotist and the hypnotized form a group of two (127). But do they? Can the group ever collapse into a relation of two? Even a multiple of two? Given what the rest of the essay reveals about the dependency of identificatory relations on an external figure, given that the lateral bond is spectralized by and for the members of the group/*Masse*, who are linked with each other along a lateral axis, in anticipation of the opprobrium or the affection of the leader, does it not make sense to think of the hypnotist as a kind of third, or at least as a figural substitute for the third? This third would be nothing other than the principle of the social, as structural anthropology (and Lacanian psychoanalysis) teaches us. If this is so, then the uncanny resemblance between the leader and the hypnotist need not depend on the origin myth of a primal horde and the insurrection of patricidal sons; rather its uncanniness consists in the repetition of a narrative mythification in which the social relation is misrecognized as a multiplicity of dyads. Perhaps all contractual models of society participate in this misrecognition. And this may be why, today, those forms of mass society linked to the cult of the leader, which relation was once associated with totalitarian polities and command economies, erupt so frequently in market-based and liberal democratic regimes. Reading Freud's essay in our own time, it now appears that the identification of the leader with the hypnotist and the group with the dyad was itself a displacement, or a repression of the linkage between contractualism and certain forms of the mass and cults of personality—the kinds that showed themselves on January 6, 2021.

Since the first decades of the twentieth century, the cult of the leader has typically been linked to totalitarianism, whether in fascism (Italian fascism under Mussolini and German Nazism under Hitler), or state socialism (the Soviet Union under Stalin, Cuba under Castro, or China under Mao). The personal proper name that signifies these historical epochs is evidence of such thought. Even the third way, Yugoslavia's 'socialism with a human face,' had Tito. However, the effort to link totalitarianism to the cult of 'The Leader' and to render this couplet as the other of liberal democratic form required the bracketing of other nationalist formations in which analogous cults emerged, whether in anti-colonialist nationalisms (for example, India under Gandhi), militarist populisms (Argentina under Peron), or sacral monarchies (Thailand under King Bhumipol). It is now clear that capitalism can accommodate any and every political form—from absolute and constitutional monarchies, to liberal democracies, welfare sates, and single-party states of an ostensibly socialist type. So too cults of the leader.

If we cannot make a causal argument linking political form and the cult of the leader to a particular economic logic, what remains for historical analysis? It is often believed that the losses claimed and lamented by contemporary white supremacists in the United States are historically recent—and this is true on all sides of the political spectrum. Civil rights legislation, economic displacement from presumptive access to the middle class and property ownership, policies aimed at mitigating police violence, gender equity, and phenomena like the Black Lives Matter movement and even Critical Race Theory, are adduced in these gestures. But the primal loss of white supremacism is already contained in the elevation of equality to an ideal. In the United States, this concept is identified with the end of slavery and its surrogate forms (even if emancipation has yet to produce real equality).

Slavery and especially chattel slavery was, of course, a structure of cheap, verily free labor. (Its cruelty cannot be fathomed here.) Anything that could mitigate its profit-generating capacities was dissuaded, at the level of the structure's logic. But the end of slavery, or rather its displacement through 'liberation' and emancipation into contractual labor, apprenticeship, and indenture, was not merely the loss of economic opportunity for former slavers.[13] Because chattel slavery in the Americas had worked on the basis of a repudiated maternal function—that function which promotes siblingship—the end of slavery also threatened to end the bar on the lateral solidarity among sisters and brothers. Now, a certain history of psychoanalysis counterposes the siblingship enabled by the maternal gaze (which need not be grounded in biological femaleness, however that is defined) and the politically potentiating fraternity enabled by the patriarchal gaze. This subordination of maternally-enabled siblingship to paternally recognized and politically significant fraternity is among the core values of white supremacy and that which is most challenged by the end of slavery and segregationism, and the rise of Black leaders in the United States. But an analysis of developments in South Africa can show us how the principle by which the political possibility of siblingship was

---

[13] The 'liberation' effected by the British ban on the trade (1807-8) and on slavery proper (Britain, 1834; USA, 1867) were the result of multinational efforts, stewarded by Britain but taking different forms in the Indian and Atlantic Ocean and the nations bordering on or islanded within them. Mandatory apprenticeship and indenture functioned as the alchemical agents of colonial capitalist consolidation, often extending unfreedom for the formerly enslaved. See Y. Christiansë, "At Sea in the Waiting Space: Slavery, Indenture in the Indian Ocean's Long Nineteenth Century," in *Being a Slave: Indian Ocean Slavery in Local Context*, Nira Wickramasinghe and Alicia Schrikker (eds), Leiden University Press, Leiden, 2020, pp. 149-181.

suppressed and survives is irreducible to slavery and operates in other forms of white supremacism. An analysis of those other forms can help us understand why white supremacism is ultimately a disavowal of the feminine/woman as anything other than the flesh that births. This is why the object of its most fetishistic investment in the places that were once dependent on antiBlack racism is the Black woman. This is also why its most loathed figure is the Black man as leader. As I said, we must proceed along two tracks or axes. For, the corollary of this history in which slavery and legal segregationism is displaced by the contract form of labor is one in which the mediation of white supremacist desire and hatred takes place within the monetary relation. Money, it turns out, holds at bay the failure of a difference that slavery requires and that has no ground but white supremacism itself. As Freud wrote to Fliess, describing its ambiguous function, "money is a means of unchaining slaves; that one obtains freedom in exchange for money, as one otherwise sacrifices freedom for money."[14] It is here that a psychoanalytic reading can supplement political economy, amplifying Marx's analysis of the fetish character of commodities, and explaining why the ressentiment about downward class mobility among today's white supremacists is linked to a desire for group identity *in the image of Black community*.

All the Things You Could Learn From Freud if Hortense Spillers Was Your Teacher[15]

The ideological ideal appears most often in silhouette. To understand this, I want to move from the story of hysterical schoolgirls to that of enslaved women, with the assistance of Hortense Spillers.

Slavery is first and foremost the effort to maximize profit through the transformation of people into mere productive machines. If slavery is threatened in its capacity to transform humans into commodities (not absolutely but relatively) by the claims of kinship, such as the right of a mother or father to a child, then, says Spillers, the

---

[14] S. Freud, Letter to Fliess, July 30, 1898, in *The Complete Letters of Sigmund Freud to Wilhelm Fliess, 1887-1904*, The Belknap Press, Cambridge, 1985, p. 321.

[15] I am invoking the title of Spillers' own essay, "'All the Things You Could Be by Now, if Sigmund Freud's Wife Was your Mother': Psychoanalysis and Race," in *Black and White in Color: Essays on American Literature and Culture*, University of Chicago Press, Chicago, 2003, pp. 376-427.

destruction of kinship, including patriarchal kinship, is demanded by the profit motive which is at best attenuated by the reticence of the 'good' slave master to separate mothers and children. Spillers turns to Claude Meillasoux for anthropological insight into the histories of slavery as it was practiced *in* West Africa, where it functioned in rivalries in political conflict, to understand what it became in the Americas: "If, as Meillassoux contends, 'femininity loses its sacredness in slavery', then so does 'motherhood' as female blood-rite/right. To that extent, the captive female body locates precisely a moment of converging political and social vectors that mark the flesh as a prime commodity of exchange. [...] this open exchange of female bodies in the raw offers a kind of Ur-text to the dynamics of signification and representation that the gendered female would unravel."[16] Reading Frederick Douglass's autobiographical narrative, Spillers postulates that the maternal gaze is necessary to transform the proximity between siblings or age-mates into kinship. We may add that this bond need have no basis in genetic substance.

Spillers's reading confers on the maternal Other the function that Freud otherwise grants to the Father and, by analogy, the leader. But it is without ressentiment and beyond the mere spiteful self-deprivation that stands for social justice and equality in his analysis. "If the child's humanity is mirrored initially in the eyes of its mother, or the maternal function, then we might be able to guess that the social subject grasps the whole dynamic of resemblance and kinship by way of the same source" (75). The same function is discerned in the father when she discusses the case of Malcolm X, who, like Douglass, is deprived of the source of kinship with his siblings after the parent's abduction and murder by white supremacists. What white patriarchy reserves for the father-as-leader has been systematically denied to Black male subjects in the American context of Spillers's account. But it is, in her analysis, the first separation from the mother that makes Black subjects so vulnerable to the further dismemberments that come with the killing and/or separation from the father. We may wish to supple-

---

[16] Spillers is quoting Claude Meillassoux, "Female Slavery," in Claire C. Robertson and Martin A. Klein, eds., *Women and Slavery in Africa*, University of Wisconsin Press, Madison, 1983, pp. 49-67. H. J. Spillers, "Mama's Baby, Papa's Maybe: An American Grammar Book," *Diacritics* 17 (2), Culture and Countermemory: The "American" Connection, Summer 1987, p. 75. All further references are in parentheses.

ment Spillers's analysis with the recognition that, in many African contexts, it is not the biological mother but the child's grandmother who confers on the child recognition and who performs much of the caregiving, but this does not change the basic structure of the argument. That argument rests on the distinction between flesh and corporeality, and asserts that female slaves forced to reproduce were, at the same time, actually deprived of gender as women because they were denied the maternal function—and in her estimation there is no female gender that is not also and at the same time an effect of patriarchal logics.

Spillers concedes the dangers of implying that female gender implies mothering, yet as she notes, gender only enters the archival record about slaves and slaving (at least in dominant discourse) in the United States through reference to women's roles as those who might give birth, so that the analysis of women in slavery comes to require and ultimately to collapse into an accounting of their reproductive capacities (a narrative of the flesh), even as women in these accounts are robbed of the maternal function. In other words, female bodily life is reduced to mere birthing capacities. It is in this light, says Spillers, that white supremacism in the US *misnames* Black woman-headed households as matriarchal. And white supremacism is still driven by a fear of Black male ascent to patriarchal authority. In this context the election of Barack Obama, a relatively culturally conservative Black president, was an event of incomparable significance for white supremacists. Because it can only grasp this ascent in terms of patriarchy and the racialized history that it otherwise represses, white supremacy may also fear its own displacement into the space of the absented gender: the female, not as maternal source of recognition, enabling the bond of kinship, but the female as *a priori*, as Luce Irigaray observes, the one before the split consciousness could erect its cruel memorial to itself in the form of the ego-ideal.[17] As Spillers notes, the 'oceanic' non-differentiated space beyond sexual difference that Freud renders as the *a priori* of gender, and that he sometimes refers to as ambiguity, was made literal in the Middle Passage. So, it is both ironic and predictable that white supremacists would perceive the so-called Black mob as a threat, for the violently usurped identity and enforced reduction to in-

---

[17] L. Irigaray, *Speculum of the Other Woman*, trans. Gillian C. Gill, Cornell University Press, Ithaca, 1985.

determinacy that was effected in the Middle Passage is precisely what they imagine will recur in the contemporary real. Moreover, *they wish it*. For, it will justify their own self-defensive group formation, even if this puts them on the precipice where their opposition will metamorphose into the mimetic reproduction of their erstwhile enemies. This is where Freud's essay offers us crucial analytical tools. For, if what is at stake is not group formation per say but its capacity for organizational durability or institutionality, and if this is imagined as a function of a leader's presence or absence, then we can expect white supremacy to be most threatened by the appearance of the Black leader.

Now, Freud's account of the hysterical schoolgirls reproduces the structure in which the maternal function enabling lateral bonds among siblings is overwritten in a story of social justice that emerges from the substitution of the leader for the father who was, of course, the displacing agent of the one gendered as woman. The structure is one of both parallelism and substitution. The lateral bonds among the brothers, cultivated in opposition to the father and then validated by recognition by a substitutional leader, generates political community in Freud's mytho-analysis. In the process, the mother is left behind and the sisters disappear. Politics, in Western discourse at least, *is* fraternity.

Reading Freud with Spillers, we see that Freud has given us a model not only of the ego in the group, but of the structural relation between kinship and politics, a relation that philosophical anthropology has often conceived in narratological and historical developmentalist terms. Readers of Arendt and her heirs will recognize this narrative as the movement from oikos to polis. Reading Spillers thirty-five years after she made this argument, we learn again that this structural model, at least in the US context, is also enabled by a history of racialization. This racialization is not secondary to the logic that feminists have long discerned in the relationship between the domestic and the political as a subordination of the former to the latter and of women to men in patriarchy; it is a constitutive fact of American political formation in Spillers' analysis. In light of the insurrection of January 6, and following extended protest over the systematic but extrajudicial killing of Black people in the US—men, women, and transgendered people—this hardly comes as a surprise. But in Freud's writings, the question of race is mainly one of religious affiliation. In his published works and in his letters, race describes the ethno-religious codification that separates Jews from Christians and he laments the racialization of science, by which he means the denigration of argument on the basis of an author's identity. But race derives from the transmission of historically accumulated knowledge at the level of the group unconscious in his writings. His text must therefore be read for what is between the lines as much as for the crude metaphors of darkness that he takes from the grab-bag of colonial discourse. This means reading him in context, which also means reading him out of context, for the scene of his writing was one of radical decontextualization, where the violent wrenchings away from home entailed by slavery were generalized and technologized. Dislocation also entered the phantasmagoria of the worlding world in dreams of travel and in the peripatetic itineraries of journeying internationalists, colonial bureaucrats, and the engineers of new industrial utopianism. One of the most important sites for the convergence of these contextualizing, decontextualizing processes and the racialization that would define Freud's century was South Africa.

More than Coincidence: The Question of a Racial(ist) Unconscious

German race science of Freud's time was concerned with difference at the level of the corporeal surface, in systems of phenotype and color—formalizing as science what emerged in centuries of colonial and slaving practice, including in German territories. The conflict between the Triple Entente (Britain, France, Russia) and the Triple Alliance (Germany, the Austro-Hungarian empire, and Italy) that emerged from the Balkans to become World War I was also fought in southern Africa, between the British-dominated Union of South Africa and the German-colonial territories of Southwest Africa. In that war, racial enmity and political affiliation were brought to the point of paroxysm, as German Southwest Africa became the scene on which German race science was acted out in genocidal violence (long before it took that form in the Fatherland). But race was complexly entangled with nation at that point. Thus, a significant alliance bound Boer nationalists, who had been vanquished by the British in the South African (Anglo-Boer) War of 1899-1902 and German Southwest Africans.

In the early days of the war, a Lieutenant Colonel of the South African Union forces, Manie Maritz, sided with the Germans and attempted to establish a secessionist republic in the image of the old South African Republic (comprising the Transvaal and Orange Free State). For the Boers, loss to the English had seemed to entail subordination to the form of governance then operative in the Cape Colony, where Black subjects, emancipated in 1834, had obtained modest access to the suffrage, when entry into the property-owning classes had been promoted as a condition for the slow assumption of Black representation. The Boers who had fled the colony at the time of the abolition, much like white supremacists elsewhere, had experienced the accession of Black subjects to full citizenship as their own loss, which was often cast in the paranoid idiom of 'Black Peril.'[18]

A declaration of martial law in South Africa led to the containment of Maritz and the Republican movement, but the white melancholia of the disaffected Boers (and not a few Englishmen) was not assuaged, and within a decade, it would find its voice in the Transvaal Report of the Local Government Commission, otherwise known as the Stallard Report. Authored by Charles Stallard, and published in the same year as Freud's *Group Psychology*, the report enunciated a regressive proposal for white separatism. It laid down the basis for a universal pass system whose stated purpose was the exclusion of Black subjects from permanent residence in urban areas.

Educated at Merton College, Oxford in the 1890s, Stallard had fought with General Smuts on the border with German Southwest Africa in 1914, just as Maritz was staging his revolt (Smuts is credited with suppressing the rebellion, and with Louis Botha, conquering the territory). His report, penned in 1921, was initially subject to intense criticism, but it had virtually become law by 1923, and the event precipitating its uptake was the Rand Revolt of 1922, when white mineworkers staged a strike against the loosening of the Color Bar, which had been justified by the Chamber of Mines on the grounds of diminished profits and a shortage of labor.[19] Spurred by fear of the displacement

---

[18] The most famous iteration of this discourse was published by Roderick Jones, a correspondent for Reuters and influential essayist as "The Black Peril in South Africa," *The Nineteenth Century and After* 37, 1904, pp. 712-23.

[19] The revolt actually commenced December 18, 1921. See N. Herd, *1922: The Revolt on the Rand*, Blue Crane Books, 1966; J. Kriker, "Women, Violence and the Rand Revolt of 1922," *Journal of Southern African Studies* 22 (3), 1996, pp. 349-72. See also I. Evans, *Bureaucracy and Race: Native Administration in South Africa*, University of California Press, Berkeley, 1997, available at https://publishing.cdlib.org/ucpressebooks/view?do-

of 2,000 white workers, the white strike metamorphosed into a fully armed insurrection, supported not only by conservative forces but by the South African Communist Party, which called on the workers of the world to "unite and fight for a white South Africa." When Smuts brought to bear 20,000 troops of the South African army to quell the uprising, on the model of his suppression of the German-sympathizing Maritz, he sealed his own fate. In 1924, he lost the election, and the following decades would see a resentful white working class become the popular base for a resurgent Afrikaner nationalism whose final victory in 1948 opened onto the formalization and constitutionalization of Stallardist principles of segregation in the form of Apartheid. The leader of that process was D.F. Malan, a Dutch-Reformed cleric and ardent cultural nationalist whose political consciousness had been spurred at least partly by the failure of Maritz's uprising.

Apartheid became the name of an exceptionalizing gesture through which a more general tendency was ascribed an artificially local provenance. Following the revelations at Nuremburg, and as the US Marshall Plan was implemented in the ostensible effort to restore Germany by deracializing and democratizing its political apparatuses, South African Apartheid became the name of segregationism everywhere. Increasingly, the identification of white supremacism with white minority rule in South Africa provided cover for the persistence of Jim Crow policies in the US, and other segregationisms elsewhere—in Palestine, for example. Pulsing beneath the surface of Malan's and the National Party's drive was the fear of being subordinated to the law of the other.

W.E.B. Du Bois's prediction that the twentieth century would be defined by the Color Bar was published in 1903. In 1904, Roderick Jones, a Reuters journalist, asserted that it would find its most urgent rationale in South Africa, where he said the Black Peril outstripped the so-called Yellow Peril, and exceeded the 'Negro Problem' in the United States. Fearful that South Africans would learn from African Americas, who he believed had emerged from the Civil War emboldened to "strive after something beyond that to which they had been born," he believed a diminishing gap between Black and white South Africans

---

cId=ft2n39n7f2&chunk.id=ch1&toc.depth=1&toc.id=ch1&brand=ucpress;query=stallard#1.

set the stage for crisis. Reading simultaneously with Du Bois but with antithetical purposes, Jones observed that "the natives are awakening from the slumber of centuries, and there is no more remarkable feature of this awakening than the thirst for knowledge."[20] Because the Cape Colony permitted Blacks (natives) who owned property of a certain value to vote, and even to run for office, and because cash wages, much of which were coming from the mines, promised an expanding voter base, he foresaw a time in which the Black voters would determine the legislative decisions of their nation.[21]

It is in this decontextualizing context, this space of both contact and separation, parallelism and divergence, that another South African whose itinerary follows Stallard's and crosses paths with Freud's, demands our attention. Roy Campbell was an English South African whose forebears had been early settlers in Natal Colony. A lover and translator of the Portuguese imperial poet Camões, he became one of the most renowned English literary figures in his country and an apparent champion of anti-racism, before descending into spiteful national self-loathing, imperial nostalgia, and ultimately, fascism as an advocate of Francoism in Spain. There is something to be learned from considering this itinerary, which offers a cautionary tale about the difficulty of separating the white melancholia of white supremacist and humanist antisupremacist sorts.

In 1918, Campbell travelled to England hoping to attend Merton College (where Stallard had been a student). Awaiting his exams, his promiscuous reading introduced him to the emerging stars of literary modernism, though he professed contempt for the novel form and preferred Romantic lyricism and epic poetry. It was in the latter domain, with the pretentious mock epic, *The Flaming Terrapin* (1924), that he acquired his first renown. *The Flaming Terrapin* is either a long poem or a short epic of rhymed couplets and based partly on Milton's *Paradise Lost*, partly on Homer's *Odyssey*, partly on the Biblical myth of Genesis, with Noah and his ark at its center, and infused with mythic elements from nearly everywhere.[22] Above all, it owes itself to

[20] R. Jones, *op. cit.*, p. 714.
[21] R. Jones, *op. cit.*, p. 715.
[22] For a good summary of *Terrapin's* narrative arc, see T. Voss, "'The Flaming Terrapin' and 'Valley of a Thousand Hills,': Campbell, Dhlomo, and the 'Brief Epic,'" *Journal of Southern African Studies* 32 (3), 2006, pp. 449-466.

Luis Vaz de Camões's *Os Lusiados,* an epic poem describing Vasco da Gama's circumnavigation of the globe, and in particular, his passing of the Cape of Storms (South Africa). In Camões' poem, a monstrous, ghostly figure whom he names Adamastor emerges from the African landpass.[23] At once Satanic and sphynx-like, a stand in for African people and a prophetic figure of redemption, Jonathan Crewe has termed Adamastor a "heterogeneal apparition," whose status as a "punitive ghost haunting the imperial enterprise" has ensured its enduring relevance for what J.M. Coetzee called "White Writing." As Crewe observes, Campbell received this figure in the mode of disinheritance rather than inheritance, thanks to his status as a self-consciously European subject far from the European metropole. Distance from the center of power was for Campbell and many of his generation a form of abjection: "In Campbell as in others similarly (dis)placed, an intense animus towards the culture of origin and a desire for local identity co-existed with a desire to *reclaim* a share of the lost cultural goods and re-enter the realm of originary privilege."[24] The colonial curriculum into which Campbell was inducted has been described as a kind of time-warp, and may explain why his modernism was merged in an eclectic poetics that often appear profoundly antimodern. But he reads the epic heroes as modern leaders, discovering in them what Horkheimer and Adorno discovered in Odysseus, namely the ur-form of bourgeois individualism and the dream of sovereignty.[25]

I have emphasized the notion of reclamation to mark the place at which the phantom of loss inserts itself. What precisely had the settler colonist lost? And when did he become conscious of this putative loss? In England, Campbell failed his entrance exams and was never admitted to Oxford. It was in exile from the hoped-for center of power-knowledge, with his new wife, Mary, that he wrote *The Flaming Terrapin,* and during this same period, he claimed in a letter to his father, that he was reading Freud. The fact that the Woolfs' publishing house, *The Hogarth Press,* began working with Freud only in 1924, means it is likely that Campbell was encountering Freud through Ernest Jones

---

[23] J. Crewe, "The Specter of Adamastor: Heroic Desire and Displacement in 'White' South Africa," *Modern Fiction Studies* 43 (1), 1997, p. 29.

[24] *Ibid.,* p. 32. Emphasis mine.

[25] M. Horkheimer and T. Adorno, *The Dialectic of Enlightenment,* ed. Gunzelin Schmid Noerr, trans. Edmund Jephcott, Stanford University Press, Stanford, CA, 2002.

and the International Psychoanalytic Journal—or perhaps through the reviews by Leonard Woolf and the writings of D.H. Lawrence, as much as through Freud himself. Campbell would later refer to Freud and Jones in tandem, summoning their names to index what he believed, from the vantage point of his later years, was the source of civilizational demise, namely an excessive reflection on unconscious motivations and a reduction of sexual life to "mechanical fatality."[26] By this point, Campbell's reading of Freud had become nearly indistinguishable from that of Lawrence, whose *Fantasia on Psychoanalysis* he had noted in a lecture in 1925. (Lawrence's *Psychoanalysis and the Unconscious* was published in the same year as Freud's *Massenpsychologie*.) Campbell had praised Lawrence's Nietzscheanism but accused him of an "obsession" with Freudian psychoanalysis. Nonetheless he shared the sense that there is a linkage between the so-called war neuroses, problems of group formation and the question of the leader. Campbell wrote on the matter in *Voorslag*, the bilingual (English and Afrikaans) journal that he cofounded and edited with William Plomer and Laurens van der Post, and where he published a vociferous commentary on art, literature, and cultural politics.

For a brief period, *Voorslag* provided the platform for European-oriented cultural criticism in South Africa, and its name, meaning 'whiplash' in English, announced its ambition to lacerate the self-complacent liberal establishment of the time. If *Voorslag* was suffused with a sense of alienation from the metropolitan center and a desire to 're-connect' settler colonial South Africa with its culturally genetic source, it appeared relatively progressive on race matters, and Campbell, who spoke isiZulu, had apparently aspired to include African-language materials in the journal, though this never came to pass. He would later renounce his antiracism, sardonically explaining his early progressivism as an effect of "Hogarth Pressure." It is not irrelevant that Campbell's split from the Bloomsbury circle was spurred by the fact that his wife, Mary, had an extended affair with Vita Sackville-West. His later disdain for the dandyism and effete polyamorousness of the group contrasted to his praise for the muscular homoeroticism of the sailor, and stands in stark contrast to his avowal of the dandy when he was

---

[26] R. Campbell, *Collected Works*, Vol. 3, 1988, p. 64; quoted in Alannah Birch, *A Study of Roy Campbell as a South African Modernist Poet*, Doctoral Dissertation, University of the Western Cape, SA, 2013, p. 178.

yet a member of the English circle. Indeed, in *The Flying Terrapin*, dandies feature alongside 'Angel cowboys' and the heroic figures of Biblical myth as analogues to Odysseus—iconic instantiations of masculine individualism.

The autobiography that he titled *Broken Record: Reminiscences* (1934) is so redolent with white supremacy that it is hard to believe its author had once asserted that "the colour-fetish […] is the incarnation of all that is superstitious, uneasy, grudging and dishonest in our natures."[27] That statement appears in an essay entitled "Fetish Worship in South Africa," (1926) which exhibits Freud's (indirect) influence on his own thought. It also borrowed a Marxian strategy of attributing fetishism to dominant social forms in order to expose their prejudicial nature. The fetishists, in this case, were "priests, politicians, journalists and military commanders" (corresponding to Freud's institutional leaders). The piece is written in the form of a dialogue and commences by asserting that "life in this country is absolutely unconscious." It continues, "as a race, we are unconscious, utterly unconscious. There is only the race-mind, the mob-soul." In Campbell's analysis, this odd predicament, of a nation that is only a mob, which is to say a group without the capacity to sustain itself in time, was a function of the shallowness of its history and the lack of a complex division of labor. In this sense, South Africa was for him an exemplification of Freud's formless *Masse*, with the result being an incapacity to generate the kind of individual who could endure—a status he reserved for people like Gandhi and artists like himself.

At this point, the punctual conversation moves toward the question of the first World War, when Campbell assumes a simulated Nietzscheanism and a Freudian critique of disillusionment. He opposed the war, he says, for its celebration of unreasonable killing, for there can be no personal motive in war and that which is not willed cannot be the expression of reason's faculty. "I would not be at all annoyed if killing were legitimised in civil life. But to glorify this extremely dull, mechanical, unreasonable killing is absurd" (8). As for the war's supposedly civilizational mission, Campbell sneers, "it had nothing to do with civilization. The Germans were 'saving civilization,' and when we woke up five years later we found we had all been helping to destroy

---

[27] R. Campbell, "Fetish Worship in South Africa," *Voorslag* 1 (2), 1926, p. 16.

civilization. And anyway what was worth saving about it? A civilization which could not assimilate the tremendous scientific resources at its command for any better purpose than to make guns and torpedos deserves to have been blown to bits" (6-7).

In Campbell's reading, the only explanation for the massness of the war, then, was the amenability of the mass to persuasion by mediocre leadership. Its error was thus a misrecognition of the proper function of the leader:

> Crowds and communities are actuated solely by the most primitive instincts: panic, suspicion, race-feeling, colour-prejudice, ferocity and patriotism. [...]
> What the mass-consciousness clamours for is a leader who obeys it. [...]The mass-leader only leads the mass in that he goes in front of it—between the shafts. He doesn't know where he is going—he leaves it to the mass. The mass don't know where they are going—they leave it to the leader. What the mass-conscious really needs is a driver not a leader: but wherever it finds one it becomes panic stricken and either nails him to a cross or poisons him as it did Socrates or drives him mad as it did Nietzsche.
> [...] Our leaders compete with each other in mediocrity: the leader who can make the greatest compromise with popular opinions is the one who gets most power: he becomes the incarnation of average mentality. ... The intellectual power of a community is not increased by numbers, for all the more individualistic elements in a crowd conflict and neutralize one another: it is only the emotional power which is increased by numbers, for emotions are contagious.

Campbell concludes by writing, "The mob passes: the individual remains" (18). It is clear that the leader is simply the apogee of bourgeois individualism. There is no concept of leadership per se, of identificatory dynamics or the lateral bonding enabled by recognition from without. We are a long way from Freud's insistence that the contagion of emotions is born of an identificatory gesture, and a desire to be in the same place as the one with whom the subject identifies. Yet Campbell agrees with Freud on the loss of subjective autonomy and faculties of judgment as definitive attributes of the mob/*Masse*. And, by the end of the glib essay, he has embraced Freud's idioms and transformed the observation that groups think in images, into a vision of the 'mob' as a phantasmagoric machine, as morbid as it is vivid: "The death-instincts in the mob are quite as strong as the life-instincts. No one can be clean and sane who submerges himself in the nightmares and dreams of the mob-psyche—for they are all dreams, illusions, nightmares—your wars and colour questions." What stands out in retrospect, given Campbell's later avowal of the most extreme colorism, is his identification of race-consciousness with the phenomenon of the mob—that thoughtless group which, if not leaderless then at least lacks a good leading idea. White supremacy is not ideational in this sense, but rather an instinctual tendency unmanaged and unsublimated. Below the level of representation, it is somehow pre-political, and possibly antipolitical: "Now fear and suspicion are the two emotions most easily generated in mass-consciousness, and wherever there is the slightest motive for these emotions they take possession of everything. The crowd is always terrified of leaving anything in the balance and must always have some wretched ideal to tie its nose to. 'White South Africa' is one of these ideals."[28]

For white identified African readers (though surely not for Black readers), Campbell's analysis of the South African white community as being functionally unconscious, a mass suffering from what resembled permanent war neurosis, was somewhat scandalous in its moment, arriving just as Stallardism was being transformed from a policy dream into a fully bureaucratized apparatus of segregationism. And as already noted, that policy legitimated itself precisely by invoking the specter of unmoored and impoverished Black masses in the city. But this figural narrative is not yet a logic. Campbell's account suggests that Stallardists were enacting something akin to mimetic desire, projecting on Black subjects the phantomatic image of their own group being—which is to say their incapacity to bring themselves into consciousness, and thus adherence to law. In doing so, he suggests, they substituted the idea of white South Africa for the recognition that they felt had been withheld from the European metropole. But it remained oblivious to the socio-economic forces that were also nourishing segregationism.

---

[28] R. Campbell, "Fetish-Worship," *op. cit.*, p. 14.

The Cost of Equality Beyond the Mob

Campbell's borrowings from Freud are often caricatures. Missing from his account of the racial unconscious is any reference to familial structure or psychodynamics of the individual subject. It misses the story of how bonds are formed among the members of the racial group; it naturalizes race while dismissing it. This is why, reading his intervention alongside the Stallardism that it seems to condemn, we learn to read Stallardism *and* Freud differently. Stallardism shows us why we must invert Freud's formula in order to grasp the truth of his analysis. Freud tells us that the group can only be understood by way of analogy with the individual psyche, and that the logic of the family provides the paradigmatic framework for grasping what is a political phenomenon, although this political dimension only becomes visible in the moment of its collapse. In fact, the horror driving the Stallardists was that Black subjects would claim their place as equals alongside whites, in the field of labor and in social life more generally. The fear of a kinship emerging between equals makes no sense in this context if the point of reference is the patriarchal family, narrowly understood. Rather, the threat to which the Stallardists responded with their generalized pass-system, such as one frequently finds in post-slaving societies (which refuses freed labor any true right of mobility), was of lateral bonds enabling a political community. Patriarchy, as described by Freud, assumes that such fraternal bonds of this sort emerge in the public sphere and are nourished as the stepchildren of recognition emanating from the leader. In this process the maternally conferred alliances of kinship are subordinated. It is the continuity between authority in the household and authority in the public sphere that Stallardists wanted to curtail—for Blacks.

South Africa was not a post-slaving society in the sense that the US was. There was certainly slavery in South Africa, especially in the Cape Colony, and the Great Trek of the Boers, following abolition, was partly motivated by a desire to maintain slaves. But the majority of Black subjects in South Africa are not descendants of slaves, and the dominant class was a numerical minority. Above all, the capitalist, mainly white classes in South Africa *used* the Black family as an instrument of reproduction; the state and capital intervened in it, differentially, along generational and gendered axes to suppress wages, but they did not foreclose it or even disavow it, as was the case in chattel slavery in the Americas. Yet, both systems converged in their aspiration to render Black women's reproduction a mere matter of the flesh. We may bring Achille Mbembe's observations about necropolitics and the disposability of African labor to bear on Fernando Pessoa's delirious surrealism here, but only by supplementing the critique of biopolitical modernity with an analysis of gender. For, it is not that "mankind is a postponed corpse that breeds," but that Black womanhood was treated as such.[29] The severance of familial bonds, though risked by migrant labor, was not akin to that achieved in the Americas. Precisely because they wanted and needed Black households to function as the sites of social reproduction (saving racial capital from this responsibility and permitting the suppression of wages), they permitted and encouraged the illusion of Black patriarchal authority, so long as it was contained within the domestic sphere. The pass system therefore aimed to sever the link that might have allowed for the metamorphosis of domestic kinship into political fraternity. When the pass laws were extended to women, they performed an analogous severance for women, but whereas the severance deprived men of status and the patriarchal function in the political sphere, it deprived women of the maternal function in the domestic sphere, by keeping migrant laboring women in their places of employment, often great distances from their mandated places of residence (in reserved territories variously called reservations, homelands, and bantustans) to ensure that the maternal function would be fulfilled not by birthmothers but by grandmothers and others. While grandmothers did indeed assume this role, and continued to fulfill it throughout the century while sustaining a great deal of Black life with enforced care-giving that is often naturalized as culture, the Stallardists' efforts ultimately failed—though not without inflicting grave wounds. Or rather, Black people and other racially minoritized subjects, with their allies, managed to produce political community despite the brutalized conditions and against the backdrop of forced separations that so mutilated domestic life in the effort to foreclose political community. Indeed, these separations were the flip side and the very medium of that racial separatism that goes by the Afrikaans name Apartheid. That Black political communities emerged

---

[29] A. Mbembe, "Necropolitics," trans. Libby Meintjes, *Public Culture* 15 (1), 2003, pp. 11-40. F. Pessoa, *A Little Larger Than the Whole Universe: Selected Poems*, ed. and trans. Richard Zenith, Penguin, New York, 1998, p. 326.

alongside and without mitigating the complicitous violence toward women that had been nurtured by colonialism, which in turn hijacked and intensified a patriarchal violence that preceded it, must give us pause—and this fact is the subject of both political activism and feminist theoretical interrogation in South Africa.

If we want to grasp the psychodynamics of white supremacism in South Africa at this time, in order to understand some of the reasons why it is so compatible with the specific logics of market economies, and hence if we want to understand why it comes back again, now, we can perhaps do no better than to read the pages of *Abantu-Batho*, the newspaper in which it was so rigorously analyzed by Black writers, thinkers, poets, and politicians who were also the contemporaries of Freud and Campbell.

Literary critical and political journalism was not the sole purview of the anxious white liberals. Several significant African-language publications provided platforms in which isiZulu, isiXhosa, Sesotho, and Setswana speakers engaged the issues that were so concerning Campbell, including those of literary production, translation, public events, theological developments, and the pass-systems through which segregationism was being implemented—systems that many African writers identified as an effort to institute slavery. Among them, the Cape-based *Imvo Zabantsundu*, edited by John Tengo Jabavu, which is credited with the successful drive to relax the pass laws in the Cape Colony.[30] Beginning in 1903, *Llange Lase Natal*, founded by John Langabilele Dube (who was the first president of the African National Congress), anchored the Zulu-language public sphere of Natal. *Abantu-Batho*, otherwise known as 'The People's Paper' (Abantu-Batho means 'The People'), was the more radical publication. It featured robust debate and commentary in several languages. All published poetry and other literary works, and all were sustained by advertising. They all also printed commentary on World War I, and the contributors to *Abantu-Batho* in particular were concerned with its diagnostic capacities and consequences for race relations, drawing from the imagery of the trenches an iconography for the segregationism that otherwise func-

---

[30] T. Couzens, "History of the Black Press in South Africa 1836-1960," Johannesburg, University of the Witwatersrand, Institute for Advanced Social Research, Additional Research Paper, n.d., p. 10.

tioned through bureaucratic procedures and brutally violent policing. In 1920, the journal's editor, R.V. Selope-Thema, wrote bitterly about the "barbed wires and trenches which the white man has established along the Colour Line in order to protect his 'mental superiority' which, alas, is incapable of competing against the 'inferior mentality' of the African without the protection of oppressive and repressive legislation, machine guns, tanks, bombs and poisonous gas."[31] The recognition that the end of the war had seen the resurgence rather than the amelioration of white supremacism in South Africa was not unrelated to the forces in the United States, where returning Black soldiers had mistakenly believed that they would be accorded comparable treatment and if not the equivalent status of their white compatriots, at least an elevation from mere servitude.[32] As Freud had noted, the soldier's reduction to metonym for the nation when perceived from without (in conflicts among national war-machines), worked to mitigate the hierarchies otherwise typical of the chain of command. And this equalization, born of exposure to the other's gaze, was the hoped-for well from which the waters of anti-segregationism might otherwise have flowed. In South Africa, that possibility was disavowed and actively suppressed by the creation of the *Jong Suid Afrika* movement (in 1918) and then the fascist Afrikaner Broederbond (in 1920), a secret fraternal organization dedicated to Afrikaner national interests and the prevention of poor whitism. A related women's organization, namely the Afrikaanse Christalike Vrouevereniging (the Afrikaans Christian Women's Movement, or ACVV) had been founded in 1904 (at the time

---

[31] R.V. Selope-Thema, "'Within the Ambit' *Abantu-Batho* February-March 1920," reprinted in *The People's Paper: A Centenary History and Anthology of* Abantu-Batho, ed. Peter Limb, Wits University Press, Johannesburg, 2012, p. 428. Selope-Thema's article begins with a citation of Booker T. Washington, and the era was marked by vigorous exchanges between the US and South Africa, along several routes, including Garveyism and, via Charlotte Maxeke, a combination of Du Boisian criticism and Christian Zionism. *Abantu-Batho* was generally positive toward the American efforts, but expressed concerns that Garveyites and African Americans did not always themselves ally with South African Blacks when in the country, and often sought exemption from the pass laws that otherwise restricted local subjects.

[32] Among the most grotesque enactments of this disavowed equality occurred on December 15, 1918, when Charles Lewis, a Black veteran of World War I, was lynched in Tyler Station, Kentucky while wearing his uniform and claiming the rights and protections of a soldier. He had been charged with robbery but was murdered for challenging white authority.

of Jones's intervention), but it was restricted to charitable activities and in this manner, had circumscribed the domain of its own intervention at the limit, beyond and beneath the political sphere proper—even if its goal of "white uplift" allied it with the overtly politicized project of the Broederbond.[33] An analysis of these organizations is beyond the scope of this essay, but we can note that the Broederbond's privileged rhetoric of fraternity and its concern to prevent downward class mobility among whites does not distinguish the Afrikaner movement from related tendencies in the rest of white South Africa; rather, it marks the point of their convergence. The Broederbond or the brotherhood is thus not merely an ethno-national organizationl moniker. It is the name of a political community premised on the foreclosure of Black subjects. That is to say, the Broederbond names a fraternity of the same. By virtue of its racialization, it not only belongs to that tradition oriented by the "schematics of 'affiliation'" in the *"familial, fraternalist*, and thus *androcentric* configuration of politics" [...] but it has encircled itself and fortified itself against inclusion, has made itself in the mode of exclusion.[34]

In that same moment that Freud's essay joined the anxious efforts to theorize the massification of society, and as the 'Colour Bar' became the form of appearance of white supremacist melancholia over the loss of inequality, there appeared an article in *Abantu-Ba-*

---

[33] Leslie Witz has argued that the ACVV "were also extending and defending their operations beyond the realm of the home" and that their efforts aimed to "incorporate the private domain of mothering into the service of the volk." Nonetheless, they actively embraced the subordination of this maternal function, identified with the reproduction and stabilization of racialized familial life, to the patriarchally generated brotherhood orienting the polis. See *Apartheid's Festival: Contesting South Africa's National Pasts*, Indiana University Press, Bloomington, 2003, p. 121. On the mother figure in Afrikaner nationalism, see Y. Christiansë, "Sculpted into History: The Voortrekker Mother and the Gaze of the Invisible Servant," *New Literatures Review* 30, special issue "Decolonizing Bodies," ed. Sue Thomas, Winter 1995, pp. 1-16.

[34] J. Derrida, *Politics of Friendship, op. cit.*, viii. It is against such exclusionary fraternity and in the name of radical friendship, which nonetheless appears "on stage with the features of the brother," that Jacques Derrida proposes to "dream of a friendship which goes beyond this proximity of the congeneric double" He adds, "The concept of politics rarely announces itself without some sort of adherence of the State to the family, without what we will call a *schematic* of filiation." The question of the brotherhood is "valid for all 'political regimes'," he argues, but especially for democratic ones and those modelled on the French revolutionary tradition that conjoins in its slogan the otherwise incommensurable terms of liberty and equality, on one hand, and "fraternity" on the other.

tho by one W. Gumede, describing a report from the Native Commissioner. Titled "Summ School e-Cabhane: An address by Jabavu," it describes a speech by Davidson Don Tengo Jabavu, son of the renowned Cape editor of *Imvo Zabantsundu,* the writer and politician invoked by Jones.[35] A Tuskegee influenced, mission-educated member of the emerging intelligentsia, DDT Jabavu was as widely known for his speech-giving tours as he was criticized for his political compromising.

In this speech, Jabavu relayed two stories, one from South Africa and one from the United States. In both cases, a Black person resides near a white person who despises him. Both are the recipients of relentless "nastiness," including not only epithets but beatings. In both cases, the Black man refrains from responding in violent kind. But over time, the Black men are able to produce a surplus of goods— in the first case, a garden of cabbages and tomatoes "and other things that are liked by the whites," in the second case, chickens and pigs, sought after by a hungry white girl "who had run out of food." After the whites had learned that the Blacks could produce surplus that the whites desired and for which they would pay, the white attitudes changed. Jabavu, as reported by Gumede, says they earned the "respect" of the white people. Jabavu's moral: "If you cultivate the soil and get much food you will become the respected on earth, because, as you know, the teeth do not rest?" The gloss tells readers that this means "all people must eat" (451).

In the structure of this relayed story, respect accrues to the one who is able to produce in excess, but only because that excess can become the object of an exchange mediated by money. After relaying these stories, Gumede reported, "he [Jabavu] said that the trouble was that we had none of the things which the whites had not" and the translator adds the following clarification: "We had none of the things they required" (452). Jabavu then asks, "How can we expect white people to respect us if we have nothing to attract them to us?" (452).

---

[35] John Tengo Jabavo had edited the first isiXhosa newspaper, *Sigidimi SamaXhosa* (The Xhosa Messenger) and founded another, namely *Imvo Zabantsundu.* Davidson took over the editorship of *Imvo Zabantsundu* when his father died. Davidson Jabavu was not always disapproved by *Abantu-Batho.* The paper had celebrated his arrival back in South Africa after ten years' absence, in 1915, when he became the first Black professor in a teacher's college. "Native College Staffing, *Abanto-Batho,* February 1915," in *The People's Paper,* pp. 360-1.

Initially, the white characters in these parables seem to treat Black people as though they are radically different, and beyond any reciprocity. Moreover, this difference seems linked to their belief that these Black people lack what the whites have. As such, it would be a mere case of presumptive inferiority. But Jabavu does not say this. He says rather that the Blacks lack what the whites lack. That is to say, the white denigration of the Black men rests on the *resemblance*, not the difference, between the white and Black figures. It is not that the whites have more (though they surely do at this moment in time), but that they both lack the means for self-sufficiency. Like the bondsmen, the masters are incomplete and incapable of self-satisfaction. Instead of alterity, then, the Blacks appear to white supremacists of the narrative as mirrors of their own lack. This is why the whites of the story hate them. Jabavu goes on to remark that when Blacks have what whites do not, they become not only worthy of recognition, but are granted honorifics (called "Mr." for example). Whites then make their monetary obeisance, submitting themselves and their requests to be satisfied at the risk of rejection.

One could read this whole scene through recourse to some transhistorical theory of desire rooted in '*the* subject's' constitutive lack—except that it is not enough for the Black subjects in this story to have what the whites lack, they must agree to *sell* it. They do not give it. Only insofar as money mediates the relation does recognition operate. In South Africa, as elsewhere in the imperial world, the intense libidinalization of money and the monetary relation is linked to a demand that Black workers both submit to the machinery that generates money and thence capital, and *not* accumulate it themselves. The vast and mutating legislative engine centered in pass laws was developed specifically to prevent this latter possibility.

The structure of desire here (which is never the same as any individual's desire) is not one in which Blacks are radically other than whites (though whiteness is positioned as Other to Blackness from its own vantage point) but rather, one in which only money can secure a difference that is constantly threatening to disappear. Indeed, it was this very possible disappearance that exercised Jones, because it was *both* the means for excluding Black subjects from the vote under then-existing legislation, *and* of their getting access to it. But even that slender possibility was structured by sexual difference, as would be exposed by Charlotte Maxeke and the women who protested their own inclusion under the pass laws on the grounds that admission to the space of Black humanity—the fraternity at once summoned and fore-closed by the passes—could only subject them to patriarchal violence precisely because, via the complicities between *different* patriarchies, it would produce a fraternity among men in opposition to them as Black women.[36] These Black women objected to the universalization of the law on the grounds that the inspection process could not be experienced similarly by men and women. They and the specular gaze of the colonial state to which they would be subject were always already sexualized. And they feared the gazes of the Black policemen and not only those of the white purveyors of passes, who not infrequently demanded sexual favors in exchange for them.

Jabavu's closing concession, that there is no other way than to participate in the white-dominated capitalist economy, represents the position of the break-away faction which, leaving *Abantu-Batho* behind, accused its editors of driving people "over the edge," toward striking, insurrection, or worse: a mob that would solicit violent suppression by well-armed colonial authorities. Yet, the only such mob that had appeared in recent memory was that of the striking white mineworkers who, on the eve of 1922, had taken up arms to prevent the access by Black miners to the ranks of skilled workers, a possibility that the white strikers read in the idiom of their own displacement and substitution.

Repetition-Compulsion: Another Lost Generation?

It is hardly necessary to quote the Alt-Right purveyors of "replacement theory," to discern the rhymes, repetitions, and apparent resemblances between the position of the white supremacist strikers of 1921-2, and the insurrectionists of 2021. Nonetheless, as I indicated at the opening of this essay, the task of historical analysis is to grasp the *apparent repetitions* as occasions for making the past illuminate the present *not only in its origins and thus as continuities, but in its differences.* If this lengthy, but still abbreviated, history of South African experiences with white supremacism *before* Apartheid serves any

---

[36] I have discussed the women's pass protests at length in "We're Ground Underfoot: Movements without Mobility," in *Unstable Ground: The Lives, Deaths and Afterlives of Gold in South Africa*, MS in preparation.

purpose, it will be to demonstrate the differences within and between antiBlack racisms in a manner that allows us to see their globalization as something related to but also exceeding Americanization. I want now to return to the other issue posed at the outset of this essay, namely that of a possible affinity between the melancholias of both white nationalists and their liberal and progressive critics. To do so requires that we take cognizance of the changed status of the mass in political discourse. For in that century between 1921 and 2021 is the entire history of the mass's totalization. And such totalized massification is, simply, death. The problem of our contemporaneity is how not to mourn this death, how to retrieve a framework for society that is not oriented by oneness or premised on exclusion.

Freud's effort to think the group/*Masse* in its positive potentiality was primarily conceived in opposition to the war-mongering nationalist mobs that had advocated the death orgies of World War I on one hand, and the impoverished collectives of strikers, anarchists, proletarians, and would-be revolutionaries, on the other. Both of these phenomena grew out of transformations emerging in the wake of the technological dimensions of industrial capitalism. From the early nineteenth century onward, radical thought has theorized these masses as the locus and agent of a global emancipation, and not merely the collectivity of the immiserated. This also meant avowing the destruction accompanying massification: of feudality, of bourgeois individualism, of property relations. But the avowal of revolutionary destruction is difficult for those who were the beneficiaries of the prior regime. This difficulty interested the cultural critics of the Frankfurt School, especially Walter Benjamin, Siegfried Kracauer, and Theodor Adorno. In retrospect, Adorno would invoke Benjamin and describe the project of critique, or rather the movement from philosophy to critique, as a "secularization of melancholy."[37] Such melancholy infuses the idiom in which these writers conceived of the world being surpassed by mass technology: as decay, dispersal, depersonalization, ruin, the loss of aura, and so forth. It is notable that these terms index a kind of agentless destruction rather than the punctual violence performed by

---

[37] T. Adorno, *History and Freedom: Lectures, 1965-1965*, ed. Rolf Tiedemann, trans. Rodney Livingstone, Polity, Cambridge, UK, 2008, p. 134. Quoted in Andrew McCann, "Melancholy and the Masses: Siegfried Kracauer and the Media Concept," *Discourse* 43 (1), Winter 2021, p. 150.

a revolutionary mob or the fantasy army of proletarian insurrection. It is also a leaderless destruction, effected by the force of massification rather than by any group. But in their effort to turn away from bourgeois individualism, these writers also risked proximity to it; and in focusing on destruction, they embraced loss. As Kracauer wrote, "the *capitalist production process* does not arise purely out of nature, it must destroy the natural organism that it regards either as a means or as resistance. Community and personality perish when what is demanded is calculability; it is only as a tiny piece of the mass that the individual can clamber up charts and can service machines without any friction."[38] A nostalgic humanist reaction against these developments held fast to the notion of personality, the ideal of the autonomous subject, and the romantic figuration of creative genius. It greeted the losses described by Benjamin in his Arcades Project with lamentation. But Benjamin recognized an emergent melancholy in the Left and not only in the political Right, identifying an attachment to vanished "spiritual values" as analogous to the commodity fetishist's attachment to things.[39]

The vacillation between an attraction to destruction and the ecstasy of liberatory struggle has long characterized Left political consciousness but in the post-Soviet, post-bipolar era, the lost spiritual values treated as things include the idea of revolutionary change itself. Already, twenty years ago, Wendy Brown claimed that the US Left had been overwhelmed by this same affect, and she produced a telling list of lost objects to which it had become attached:

> the losses, accountable and unaccountable, of the Left are many in our own time. The literal disintegration of socialist regimes and the legitimacy of Marxism may well be the least of it. We are awash in the loss of a unified analysis and unified movement, in the loss of labor and class as inviolable predicates of political analysis and mobilization, in the loss of an inexorable and scientific forward movement of history, and in the loss of a viable alternative to the political economy of capitalism. And on the backs of these losses are still others: We are without a sense of an interna-

---

[38] S. Kracauer, "The Mass Ornament," in *The Mass Ornament: Weimar Essays*, trans. Thomas Y. Levin, Harvard University Press, Cambridge, MA, 1995, p. 78.

[39] W. Benjamin, "Left-Wing Melancholy," in *The Weimar Republic Sourcebook*, eds. Anton Kaes, Martin Jay, and Edward Dimendberg, University of California Press, Berkeley and Los Angeles, 1994, p. 305.

tional, and often even a local, left community; we are without conviction about the truth of the social order; we are without a rich moral-political vision to guide and sustain political work. Thus, we suffer with the sense of not only a lost movement but a lost historical moment; not only a lost theoretical and empirical coherence but a lost way of life and a lost course of pursuits.[40]

In many respects, little has changed, or rather things have become more the same. Certainly, the problem of the mass has returned, in all its ambivalence. But if as Brown says, mass phenomena are now lacking in unity, movements of *both* white nationalist or supremacist sorts *and* antiracist commitments have nonetheless continued to proliferate throughout the globe.

In the shadow of twentieth century totalitarianisms, Left theoretical labors to redeem the category of the commons, the community, the multitude, and the *plus d'un* are confronted with the need to elaborate a conceptual infrastructure for collective action without, at the same time, submitting to the lure of the one, especially if it is operated by the state. Finding a basis for gathering is all the more difficult in a time when labor is itself increasingly dispersed. In the present media-technological milieu, defined by a lack of preparation for leaderless collectivity, group formations increasingly rely on technologically-generated images of themselves—in lieu of recognition by an other. One sees this in the media practices of protest movements that feature the circulation of realtime images of the group as the foundation for its sense of coherent agency.[41] These efforts concede the need for such an image or rather an imago, for those educated within the subjectifying structures of a nucleated family. In the "go-for-broke game of history,"[42] they gamble that technology can perform the functions of recognition that patriarchal society has until now distributed along the binarizing axis of the maternal and the paternal. They wager that such technology could enable the assemblage of something like siblings, before and beyond the division between sisters and brothers.

---

[40] W. Brown, "Resisting Left Melancholy," *Boundary* 2 (26), 1999, p. 22.

[41] See my 'Theses on the New *Öffentlichkeit*,' revised, *Grey Room* 51, 2013, pp. 94-111.

[42] S. Kracauer, "Photography," trans. Thomas Y. Levin, *Critical Inquiry* 19 (3), Spring, 1993, p. 435.

But here, too, we might say that the teacher or rather the function of retraining the imagination has been elided. For, in the absence of a careful reorientation of desire, in the absence of a scrupulous interrogation of all the assumptions on which family, the familiar, and the fraternal have been erected within the racialized and globally racializing history of capital, technology will not, of its own, displace the social logics in which it has emerged. It will, rather, intensify them. This is what Benjamin understood about fascism as an effort to unify the mass in an aesthetic mode, to provide it with a figure and a face.[43]

It is clear, however, that white supremacism and nationalist populism have no such hesitation—no reticence to embrace the Leader, to find satisfaction in fraternity, to experience the jouissance of submitting to the One, and to use technology for this purpose. Perhaps this is the most profound source of Left melancholy today. They, the white nationalists, have what the Left critics of authoritarianism willingly relinquished, namely the belief in and valorization of a coherence guaranteed by the leader, modelled on the father of the patriarchal family. For, in the absence of a leader-concept derived from patriarchal headship and in suspicion of the mob in which equality is often reduced to equal access to inequality (the right to accumulate wealth), solitude calls. This fact became all the more visible in the aftermath of the end of Apartheid and the election of Barack Obama. These two events called into question the necessity of thinking racial equality as simultaneously and *necessarily* a project of exiting the logics of family, and with it a model of politics as the subordination of female to male, of siblingship to fraternity, of maternal function to paternal function. Because this necessity was not adequately thought, these events, which should have constituted the bare beginnings of a struggle, were mischaracterized as endings. In fact, these events constituted the substitution by and misrecognition of the Leader for the end of inequality. In other words, Freud's lesson, which was perhaps best discerned by the teacher, DDT Jabavu, has not been learned.

---

[43] E. Cadava and S. Nadal-Melsió, "Politically Red," review of Fredric Jameson's *The Benjamin Files*, forthcoming.

Without Title

We conclude with a recognition that ending is not possible, that the interminability of the psychoanalytic session opened by Freud remains the challenge of all criticism whose object is the situation in which politics is modeled on the family and collectivity abandons itself to the leader. I will not repeat here what has been argued in the preceding pages, but I will return once again to Spillers, who writes, "Even though the captive flesh/body has been 'liberated,' [...] dominant symbolic activity, the ruling episteme that releases the dynamics of naming and valuation, remains grounded in the originating metaphors of captivity and mutilation so that it is as if neither time nor history, nor historiography and its topics, shows movement, as the human subject is 'murdered' over and over again by the passions of a bloodless and anonymous archaism, showing itself in endless disguise."[44] Spillers speaks from the margins of the American position, and I have already suggested the need to supplement this analysis with a recognition of its continuity and difference with racialization elsewhere. But let us note her phrasing again: "It is *as if* neither time nor history... shows movement." The *als ob* of Spillers's text alerts us to the fact that there has been movement, but not change, nothing that enables the perception of time's passage as the leaving behind of the past. And this incapacity to leave it behind is the very structure of melancholia.

This fact became newly available for reflection, as the anniversary of Freud's essay on mass psychology took place in the epochal non-event of a global pandemic. I refer to this slow and unrelenting catastrophe as a non-event for the very reasons that Spillers invokes the notion of stasis. If the event is that which precipitates a transformation in narratable history, then the pandemic has not so much changed the world as reveal and intensify its structural characteristics. According to a certain literalization of Freud's idiom, we might say that, revealing and intensifying the social and economic inequalities that structure vulnerability to disease and access to medical care and prophylactic as well as therapeutic medications in the US and globally, the pandemic became something like a pathogenic situation, enabling a kind of hysterical conversion in the form of white supremacist insurrections.

---

[44] H. Spillers, "Mama's Baby, Papa's Maybe," *op. cit.*, p. 68.

They were there, but they appeared anew under pandemic conditions. Once again, a pathologizing nomination is insufficient to the analytic task, which must commence rather than conclude the necessarily double session of reading, and with a recognition of a norm that has become destructive.

It is therefore instructive to recall Richard Spencer's description of the agenda of the Alt-Right, made four years prior to the insurrection. Its aim, he said, would be the acquisition for whites of what he believes Black subjects in the US already possess, namely identity: "Blacks are quite good at identity politics. They know who they are. We want that too." [45] A few years later, we can say that the insurrectionists wanted what the protestors of George Floyd's murder had. Thus, while Spencer's speech gives voice to a mimetic desire that is premised on wanting what Black subjects ostensibly have, it also reveals that the identity formation which he has in mind is born of loss. The object of white supremacist envy is this loss. In other words, white supremacy perceives its own lack, its failure to be universal, *as loss.* This fact is somewhat distinct from that noted by Juliet Hooker: "The paradox of contemporary white loss is thus that it is driven by symbolic black gains (such as the Obama presidency) that function to support the status quo of, at best, incremental change toward racial equality, accompanied by the retrenchment or slow erosion of the significant civil rights victories of the 1960s."[46] If this describes the overt discourse of white supremacy, it does not yet grasp the extraordinary reading DDT Jabavu showed, namely that it is the proximity and resemblance between the insufficiencies and dependencies in Black and white communities that leads the white supremacist to attempt to secure the perimeter of identity—effecting and policing but also concealing racial identity rather than difference, in the economic domain—and then rendering it as *a function* of race.

Was it the dream of the sovereign, as the One, the masculine one and father-leader, that brought us to this point? Spillers's *als ob* is also

---

[45] K. Mangan, "Richard Spencer, White Supremacist, Describes Goals of His 'Danger Tour' to College Campuses," *Chronicle of Higher Education*, November 28, 2016, http://www.chronicle.com/article/White-Supremacist-Describes/238515.

[46] J. Hooker, "White Grievance and the Problem of Political Loss," in *Grief and Grievance*, eds. Okwui Enwezor et al., Phaidon, London, 2021. I thank Eduardo Cadava for alerting me to this text.

the grammatical gesture of the imagination, of the opening to a future still to come. If fraternity is the idea of a leaderless group redeemed from the status of the mob, it is also the Trojan horse of patriarchy. What else might be possible? A politics of siblingship would substitute *something like* a maternal function for the leader, but it would not and could not be the mere valorization of maternity, nor the inversion of the value system that presently denigrates the feminine. One task of the present is to retrieve the term of siblingship from its imbrication in that most exclusive of units, that most conditional of unconditionalities: in what is familiarly called family, the origin of the (nationalist and white supremacist) group, as Freud well knew.

A Language of Hate: Brazil, January 2019 to December 2022
Betty Fuks

> "Words, words, and nothing more than words, as Prince Hamlet said. ... A means by which we convey our method to influence other people. Words can create an inexpressible good and also cause terrible wounds."[1] S. Freud, 1926

Gustave Le Bon, whose *Psychologie des foules* (1895) is the main reference in the essay *Massenpsychologie und Ich-Analyse*, considered hypnotic suggestion a powerful tool in the task of the State to make the people submit to its interventions. Conscious of their influence and power, the sociologist held the theory that one need only know how to handle words according to the meaning they were to be used for, since "words, like ideas, are living things."[2] That is to say, the leader should "choose well the terms of the ideological narrative, so that the most hateful things would be accepted;"[3] a thesis which Le Bon justifies by listing as examples some actions on the part of despots who, in the course of history, had invoked using popular words to command a united crowd. In 20th-century political history, the sociologist's ideas would inspire the electrifying performance of leaders such as Mussolini and Hitler. Indeed, it's possible to note such an influence in *Mein Kampf* where Hitler insists on the necessity for the National Socialist Party to adopt the word as a strategy for mass persuasion, given that "it was possible to have at hand an army of demagogues in high style to influence, through oratory, the battle against

---

[1] S. Freud, *Inhibitions, Symptoms and Anxiety*, in *The Standard Edition of the Complete Psychological Works of Sigmund Freud*, Vol. XX (1926), London: The Hogarth Press, 1975, p. 187.
[2] G. Le Bon, *Psicologia das multidões*, Martins Fontes, São Paulo, 2018, p. 101. [*The Crowd: a Study of the Popular Mind*, Dover Publications, 2002]
[3] *Ibid.*, p. 102.

the enemy."[4] The closeness of the point at which language touches the real lever of the political project of Nazi-fascist implementation of hatred of the Other appears in the following statement: "the spoken word, for psychological reasons, is the only force capable of prompting great revolutions."[5] We know how much the Führer used the power of oratory in the political field to bring about the revolt of the masses against individuals who did not fit into the identitarian definition of the "pure" race.

Today it would be impossible to think about Nazi-fascism without taking into account Freud's thesis in his *Massenpsychologie* that members of the crowd under a leader's hypnosis are so transformed that their very subjectivities are destroyed. The minds of humans, political animals, are not being commanded by a herd drive;[6] Freud makes a point of discarding the thesis of Wilfred Trotter who had defended the primary existence of the drive, insisting that it is language that keeps individuals united. Language owes its importance to its aptitude to ensure reciprocal understanding in the herd, grounding the identification of some individuals with others,[7] while all remain identified with the leader's promise to protect them from the alien.

On one point Freud agreed completely with Le Bon's analysis: "the crowd, or mass, is subjected to the truly magical power of words, which can rouse in the crowd's soul the most terrible torments and yet also allay them."[8] The contrary and antithetical effects of words had an intense impact on Freud, as we can see from the epigraph to the present essay, from the very outset of the talking cure that laid the foundation of psychoanalysis. In what he says regarding the power of words, Freud explains that the leader of the crowd uses the same technique as the hypnotist. He viewed this "hypnotic relation" as "a group formation with two members"[9] that materializes the superego's orders and obscene injunctions in the voice of the leader resonating with an imperative—"You must!" Obediently, the uncritical individuals

---

[4] A. Hitler, *Mein Kampf - Minha luta* (1925), Mestre Jou, São Paulo, 1962, p. 296.
[5] *Ibid.*, p. 293.
[6] S. Freud, *Group Psychology and the Analysis of the Ego, op. cit.*, p. 119.
[7] *Ibid.*, p. 195.
[8] *Ibid.*, p. 149.
[9] *Ibid.*, p. 190.

become "practictioners of voluntary servitude," as Rey Flaud has put it so precisely.[10]

"Language is more than blood." This sentence from the philosopher Franz Rosenzweig serves as the epigraph to the book *LTI – The Language of the Third Reich* by the philologist Victor Klemperer. It sums up the sense of a book that colorfully illuminates the way in which language was turning into a tool to identify, manipulate, and seduce the German people into ultranationalistic, xenophobic worldviews. "Language is more than (a matter of) blood." A statement with a double meaning, as Luis Sérgio Krausz points out: on the one hand it synthesizes the idea that the language in which subjects express themselves, dream, and think is the foundation of their identity, an immaterial blood heavier than their physical blood; on the other hand, it is a response to the ideology of purity of blood that barred from the language of the German people and its culture all those foreign to its supposed genealogy.[11]

Be that as it may, Klemperer's book bears witness to the way in which the ideologues of the Third Reich developed a system able to adulterate and reduce the German language to an impoverished dialect, through simplification of syntactic structures, corruption of the meaning of words, confusion of nouns and adjectives, etc. Complementary to this, they created acronyms, emblems, "watchwords," expressions that condensed the whole ideology which, through thousands of mechanical repetitions seeped "into the flesh and blood of the masses."[12] The adulteration of language was the most important piece in the reforming of German identity according to the myth of the pure and noble race, the Aryan myth. For instance, it was necessary to pervert the signifier "Jew," degrading it to the point that it was reduced to a virus. This is why it can be claimed that language as a tool of political domination promoted and ultimately guaranteed the Final Solution. Accordingly the ideologues of the Third Reich sought to turn

---

[10] H. Rey-Flaud, "Os fundamentos metapsicológicos de O mal-estar na Cultura," in *Em torno de O mal-estar na cultura de Freud*, Escuta, São Paulo, 2002.

[11] L. Sérgio Krausz, "Conciência e inconsciência do nazismo," in *Pandaemonium Germanicum*, pp. 190-196, www.fflch.usp.br/dlm/alemão/pandaemoniumgermanicum.

[12] V. Klemperer, *LTI: a linguagem do Terceiro Reich*, Contraponto, Rio de Janeiro, 2009, p. 55 [*The Language of the Third Reich. LTI – Lingua Tertii Imperii*], Bloomsbury Academic, New York, 2013.

the maleficent meaning of the term "fanaticism" into a synonym for virtue, for "intense and strong passion that inflames people's hearts, enabling them to despise death."[13] Thus spread the ideology that guaranteed individuals immunity from responsibilities and feelings of guilt.

Generally, then, the Third Reich created an extremely monotonous but calculatedly exacerbated discourse, the form of which, following Freud's intuition, was "to sustain the image of the super-strong leader amid equal companions."[14] Thus, colonizing the language of the other, the German Reich promoted and implemented a return to the mass psychology that paved the way for the cultural catastrophe of national socialism. Manipulating signifiers presumably serves to capture, dominate, and impose on all a determined world-view. As psychoanalysis insistently points out, politics always tries to forge a program offering ideological identity precisely where the subject finds itself lacking. Beyond the zeal of manipulating master signifiers, the political program of Nazism induced a state of isolation and enclosure, blocking the Otherness of language. Thus, the German National Socialist Party imposed the idiom of barbarism that, with the help of the cutting-edge science of the 20th century, made the *Shoah* possible.[15]

One could relate the Nazi effort to adulterate and corrupt language in general—and the German language in particular—to what George Orwell described in his novel *1984*.[16] There he devised "Newspeak," a fictitious idiom forged out of the destruction of existing languages, to block the emergence of opinions contrary to the totalitarian political regime. Though he wrote the novel in the postwar period, leading us to associate it with the catastrophe the world had just recently lived through, the author prophesied the advance of a technology more dominant today than ever before. For instance, in the middle of the last decade the political world was seized with alarm at the creation of new weapons of psychological manipulation—from Big Data to the algorithms—for hacking elections in many countries. These new tactics for threatening democracy are just up-to-date versions of social control for manipulating hatred against the other. It is evident that the internet is a powerful tool to protect fake news, a

---

[13] *Ibid.*, p. 112.
[14] S. Freud, *Group Psychology and the Analysis of the Ego, op.cit.*, p. 199.
[15] A Hebrew word meaning, literally, "destruction," "ruin," "catastrophe."
[16] G. Orwell, *1984*, Companhia das Letras, São Paulo, 2009.

form of propagating information that manipulates and refines the lie, one of the pillars of totalitarianism.[17] Orwell's prescience regarding the contemporary tools of technology was recently demonstrated in the actions of Donald Trump and the followers of Q-Anon during the U.S. elections, as well as in the election of Jair Bolsonaro in Brazil.

Orwell's dystopia brings us back to LTI, *Lingua Terti Imperii*, the language of fanaticism, which possessed an inflamed aesthetic allied to the use of State violence, as Peter Cohen's documentary film *The Architecture of Doom* demonstrates. The Nazi aesthetic was constructed obsessively, inch by inch, to affect and quickly goad the people to identify with the ideals of the Third Reich. The precision of the "goose steps" of troops marching to the drumbeat while holding up Party flags emblazoned with swastikas attests to the full scope of the aesthetic of death and destruction in the totalitarian German state.[18] What is immediately evident in the filmmaker's exposition is the "poisonous hatred" for the other transmitted through National Socialist ideology.

Bit by bit, nationalism destroyed the social links in Germany, exalting its essentialist and ethnocentric mark—German identity—against the State's "objective enemy," as Arendt put it.[19] This was the basis for the new religion dreamed of by the Third Reich, which was to be consecrated upon the altar of hatred and intolerance of otherness. Benito Mussolini, who received aid from Hitler starting in 1943, convinced the Italians that he would protect them from the Communist menace through vast social reforms.[20] In the Nazi regime and in Fascism, it was apparently not the dead father who grounds the origin of the paternal function in his murder, as the Freudian myth spells out in *Totem and Taboo*.[21] Rather, we find there the introduction of the

---

[17] Hannah Arendt pointed out this function of the lie in *The Origins of Totalitarianism: Part I – Antisemitism* (1951), Harcourt Brace Jovanovich, New York, 1973.

[18] P. Cohen, *The Architecture of Doom*, documentary film, 1989.

[19] H. Arendt, *The Origins of Totalitarism, op. cit.*

[20] U. Eco, *O fascismo eterno*, Editora Record, Rio de Janeiro, 2018, pp. 30-31 [*The New York Review of Books* https://www.nybooks.com/articles/1995/06/22/ur-fascism/].

[21] S. Freud, *Totem and Taboo*, in *Complete Psychological Works, op. cit.*, Vol. XIII, chapter IV. "The scientific myth of the father of the primal horde," as Freud wrote in *Massenpsychologie*, lends human voice to the concept that responds to the origin of language as systems of differences, of culture and social organizations: repression (or primal repression: *Urverdrängung*). In its terse density, the myth of *Totem and Taboo*, like any myth, introduces an inflection point: the suppression of an arbitrary figure of power by an act of

tyrannical, omnipotent father who leads the benumbed horde in the name of love, demanding unconditional loyalty and obedience of all who in their helplessness clamor to be saved from death.

The language, the discursive rhetoric, and the aesthetic of the Third Reich are all paroxysms of hatred toward the other that must be guarded against even in post-totalitarian, democratic societies. The echoes of the historico-cultural catastrophe of Nazi-fascism have scattered over the four corners of the globe in a permanent attempt at revival. In the 21st century their rumblings awaken the fear in many of us that we may be facing another resurgence of the primal horde.

The Language of Hate in the 21st Century

History repeats itself, and it does so "the first time as tragedy and the second time as farce," as Karl Marx remarked at the beginning of his book *The 18th Brumaire of Louis Bonaparte*, emending Hegel's assertion that the great deeds and the great figures of history make their stage appearances twice.[22] What we should take away from Marx's celebrated maxim is that farce doesn't cease to be tragic, farcical though it may be.

To say the least, it was embarrassing to watch the Brazilian government making use of the language and the aesthetic of the Third Reich in its declarations to the nation and in its institutional propaganda. When we reflect on the role that these modes of communication played in the ultimate extermination of Jews, homosexuals, gypsies, and the mentally ill during the Second World War, we could no longer deny how directly they had inspired Bolsonarism. Confronted with that perception, we went from the sense of embarrassment at what shames us to the unmistakable feeling of angst. As Freud observes in *Inhibition, Symptoms and Anxiety* (1926), angst is the signal referring to the traumatic situation in which danger, whether outer or inner, real danger, and the demand of the drive converge. Perhaps for this very reason angst, in Lacan's words, the one affect that doesn't deceive,[23] is

---

violence. "One day the brothers who had been driven out came together, killed the father and devoured him, and thus put an end to the paternal horde" (p. 141).

[22] K. Marx, *The Eighteenth Brumaire of Louis Bonaparte*, International, New York, 1994.

[23] J. Lacan, *The Four Fundamental Concepts of Psychoanalysis*, Seminar XI, Karnac Press, London, 1964, p. 41.

the most precise signal for psychoanalysts to attune their listening to the traumatic political moment Brazil has recently gone through.

Ever since the 2018 electoral campaign, Bolsonaro's discourse was replete with linguistic expressions directly translated from the German as well as paraphrases maintaining the essence of the destructive, racist, and militaristic aesthetic of the Third Reich. That is to say, the president's parroting of the Nazi language that led to the de-democratizing of Hitler's Germany was aimed at ensuring the imposition of a far-right political project to dominate the Brazilian people. While we may not be able to label Brazil's former president a Nazi or a fascist, nothing keeps us from categorizing him as a tyrant. A tyrant who, in his resemblance to other populist leaders, needed only to guarantee protection to the people by dividing the world into two compartments: first "us" (as in "America First"), and then "them," those different from us, and worthy as such of persecutory hatred.

It was said that Bolsonaro chose to paraphrase the Nazi jargon of *Deutschland über alles*, Germany above all, as a way to propel his candidacy and later his government. The slogan "Brasil acima de tudo" (Brazil above all) was used while he was a candidate and it's also used by the Brazilian army, clearly signifying a call to carry out his populist project. In Portuguese, the watchword "Brasil acima de tudo" was annexed to the expression "God above all"—linking the future government to the Evangelical sector. Bolsonaro found in the phrase "Brasil acima de tudo; Deus acima de todos" the guarantee for his electoral success.

More frightening still was the fact the future president used the rhetoric inherent to Nazism and racism to raise votes. We need only recall Bolsonaro's speech at the Club Hebraica, an occasion on which he compared a member of the *quilombola* (i.e., a Maroon, or fugitive slave) community to "an animal that has its body mass measured in *arrobas*"[24] and reminded his audience that "for over three and half centuries, Black people were legally traded as slaves in Brazil, traded on the basis of the body mass they displayed." Furthermore, Bolsonaro proceeded to announce the decision that, if elected, he would expel the Amazon Indians from their millennial habitat, which he would turn over to the capitalism that reigns supreme in our current stage

---

[24] A Brazilian measuring unit for weight, equivalent to 15 kg.

of civilization: "Not a centimeter's going to be marked off for an indigenous reservation or for quilombolas" (Bolsonaro, April 5, 2017). A promise that contained the notion that it's possible to steal the right of the indigenous or quilombola collectivity who reside in their territories—so similar to the appropriation of Jews' cultural goods and property that occurred in the Nazi state. No less shocking than his racist declarations was Bolsonaro's choice of venue, the house of a people that had suffered planned genocide at the hands of the Third Reich. Yet the episode, which stirred laughter and applause from the public in attendance, for the most part Jews, gave proof, at least for us psychoanalysts, that the "narcissism of small differences"[25] can reach a paroxysm in obliterating the very historical memory of those present. Any narcissistic puffing up of the ego or of a group immediately creates unawareness and ignorance of alterity.

Historically the 2018 elections legitimated a government which, from the very outset, showed itself to be antidemocratic, markedly populistic, and nationalistic. But before going deeper into this topic, I'd like to point to other episodes of the Bolsonaro government directly linked to the mimetic identification with the Nazi-fascist language and aesthetic. In a January 2020 institutional video, the then Secretary of Culture, Roberto Alvim, paraphrased the Reich Minister of Propaganda, Joseph Goebbels, indeed, even did so to Wagnerian strains. Despite the secretary's subsequent dismissal from his post, it's impossible to believe that this episode could be isolated from the government's far-right agenda. As one of the major militants in the Bolsonarist "culture war," Alvim merely confirmed that icons of Nazi-fascism feed the social symptom of hate speech against art and thought in Brazil. This sort of grim exaltation regarding culture may also be identified in President Bolsonaro's choice to appoint as president of the Palmares Foundation, an institution allegedly created to protect Black culture, someone who declared in social media that slavery had been "beneficial for the descendants of African populations," despite being himself one of those descendants.

Further on in this circuit of horror, the ex-chancellor Ernesto Araújo compared social isolation measures to combat the Covid-19 pandemic to the extermination camps in which millions were mur-

---

[25] S. Freud, *Civilization and Its Discontents* (1930), *Standard Edition*, XXI.

dered for their ethnic identities, sexual orientations, ideological choices, etc. The chancellor's absurd analogy revealed the government's intention to confuse the Brazilian people. The action of discrediting the recommendations for isolation from the World Health Organization and other scientific institutions subverted their message to protect against the spread of the virus. In the Bolsonarist crusade, the speeches of Alvim and of Araújo were not isolated instances: As late as 2020, the Secretary for Communication (Fábio Wajngarten) published a video, shared by the president, with a translation of the phrase inscribed over the entrance gate to Auschwitz: *"Arbeit macht frei"* (Work liberates). The association between the video and recollection of the extermination camps was not lost on the press and public entities. The secretary argued how unlikely this reading was, given the fact that he himself is Jewish, a justification both inappropriate and obscene. The fact that the secretary should have evoked his origins to defend the use of the phrase "Work liberates"—"O trabalho liberta"—revealed him as a citizen who wants to be 'above suspicion,' subscribing to the phrase with which the Nazi executioners concealed what really was going on in the extermination camps.

Finally, if Klemperer's book contains precious hints for thinking and reflecting on the Brazilian government's mimicry of the language and the aesthetic of the Third Reich, it isn't hard to recognize courses of action of a politics rapidly heading toward the worst. But the choice of the path that steeped the 20th-century world in blood and suffering isn't unique to Brazil. These days it is "eternal fascism," in keeping with philosopher Umberto Eco's analysis in 2008 of the state of mind of many of "democracies" scattered around the planet.[26] *"Ur*-Fascismo," a notion he coined to demonstrate the omnipresent traces of fascism in culture, reveals the fact that if, on the one hand, Fascism was extinguished at the end of Wold War II, on the other hand, many of its traits persist. One of the firmest proofs of Eco's thesis are the statements and acts of hyper-nationalistic leaders, among them Hungary's presdent Víctor Orban, Poland's prime minister Mateusz Morawieck, and the Philippines' recent president Rodrigo Duherte, heads of states who threaten to dissolve the rule of law.

---

[26] U. Eco, *op. cit.*

Another trait of Ur-fascism is the *cult of tradition*, which long predates fascism, having emerged, according to Eco, out of the reaction to classical Greek rationalism at the height of the Hellenistic era. The reactionary and conservative ascent of the Neo-Pentecostal sects which have been spreading for decades throughout Brazil provided the Bolsonaro government with a major ally in its efforts to cripple the advance of knowledge and encourage traditionalism. In this sense, Bolsonarist obscurantism (or anti-science) foreshadowed something similar to what Freud saw coming on the eve of the Second World War. In a private conversation with Marie Bonaparte, in the face of the princess's attempt to convince him that antisemitism was little more than an ill left over from the Dark Ages, Freud insisted: "Just wait, we're going to see the terrible, offensive return of religious obscurantism."[27] Borrowing these words from the creator of psychoanalysis, we can affirm that the anti-scientific offensive against the intelligentsia and the universities of Brazil by its former president attested to the return of one of the most perverse traits of fascism. "Flat-earther"-style denial of global warming is just one of the stances aimed at disqualifying and attacking scientific knowledge, philosophy, and the human sciences, denying and rejecting them, and covering them up in traditionalist and religious claims.

The reaction to diversity, another trait of Ur-fascism, now assails Brazilian reality. A typical characteristic of régimes that wage intense opposition to critical analysis and the paradoxes of the world of ideas is the exertion of repression and control over sexuality, as Eco points out. If the ideologues of Nazi-fascism deemed homosexuality a pathology and accordingly sent thousands of males and females accused of it to the gas chambers, today we found the previous head of the Ministry of Women, the Family, and Human Rights, Damares Alves, repudiating and publicly attacking any "sexual choice" other than heterosexuality. Furthermore, there is a veritable war being waged against Gender Studies, with a concurrent disregard of anything that psychoanalysis and civil rights movements might have to say on the topic. Alves proposed suppressing the subject of desire, advocated strict and hierarchical sexual codes, and argued for a possible "gay cure." Such a

---

[27] Quoted in E. Roudinesco, *História da Psicanálise na França I (1895-1939)*, Zahar, Rio de Janeiro, 1996. [*Histoire de la Psychanalyse en France* 1 *(1895-1939)*], Éditions du Seuil, Paris, 1986.

proposal revealed the Bolsonarist government's structural aversion to the different social registers of multiculturalism.

The Minister (who is a minister in another sense as well: an Evangelical pastor) offered the striking defense that sexual abstinence is the only suitable means to protect against premature pregnancy. She ruled out any sort of sexual education as a solution to this problem affecting so many teenagers, a large majority of whom come from the poorest sector of the population. The minister was proposing to bring morality back to society by authoritarian means: to undo the advances in civilization with regard to the exercise of sexuality, urging a broader retreat from physical intimacy until maturity. To achieve her goals, the minister, who defined herself as "terribly Christian," appointed a woman lawyer avowedly opposed to abortion, even in cases of rape, to the position of director of the Department of Women's Dignity, at the very moment when a majority of Brazilians said they felt sorry for the ten-year-old girl made pregnant by the uncle who had been abusing her already for four years.[28] The rallying cause of catechizing women and getting them to accept a rapist's violence as divine purpose can be likened to the Nazis' decision not to allow gay women raped by Hitler's soldiers to abort.

Clearly there was nothing accidental about the culture war launched by the Ministry of Education against the universities, the research centers, and the schools of Brazil. Knowledge has to be monitored by the State for, if left unchecked, scientific investigation can produce findings and opinions contrary to the ideology the State wants to impose. Along the same lines, it accused professors, without proofs, of wreaking havoc in the form of "pot plantations" and "drug kitchens." The paranoia stirred up here was justified by the fact that the Ministry wanted to change the rules of the Republic to banish the "leftist paradise" from the country. For fascists, the relation to culture is always a war, as Eco reminds us, quoting the inflammatory statement attributed to Goebbels: "Whenever I hear someone speak of culture, I want to pull out my gun."[29]

---

[28] According to the official 2021 statistics of the Brazilian Forum for Public Safety (Fórum Brasileiro de Segurança Pública), every 15 minutes in Brazil, a girl under age 13 is raped, and 76 percent of the rapes filed with the police were perpetrated by close relatives or family acquaintances.

[29] U. Eco, *op. cit.*, p. 49.

We could find the same deadly thrust of that statement by the master-mind of the great book-burning at the University of Berlin in 1933 in the acts of our former minister of the environment, and the minister who succeeded him, who didn't hide the government policy aimed at destroying the Amazon, the cradle of indigenous culture. Beyond prompting devastating losses to health and the environment, fires in the Amazon jungle, "the lungs of the world," have been slowly decimating the indigenous peoples who are their traditional guardians. Add to this state of things the total absence of protection from Covid-19, and you had a populace "on the brink of a genocide," as the great photographer Sebastião Salgado put it in an open letter to Bolsonaro that was further signed by various international celebrities.

Finally, it is necessary to recall that the deliberate strategy of adulterating the Portuguese language, the strategy of Bolsonaro's own government, bred fear and indignation. For instance, the word for "torturer," *torturador*, was given a new meaning: "hero." Colonel Carlos Brilhante Ustra, sentenced for torture by Brazilian justice, was presented by the president of the republic as a hero and, as such, was elevated to the rank of marshal, according to the press. In the violent shift in meaning of key words lay one of the most destructive linchpins of the Bolsonaro government: it's not a matter of an effort to snuff out the marks of history, like those of a crime. As we read in Freud's *Der Mann Moses und die monotheistische Religion*, the difficulty lies not in carrying out the act, but in eliminating its traces.[30] Bolsonarism makes no attempt to "alter appearances," or to "place elsewhere, dislocate" the truth of murder. It's interested in *excluding* the truth of murder, banishing it beyond the country's borders and doing so for all the generations of Brazilians.

Beyond efforts to manipulate the language and the history of the Brazilian people, Bolsonaro established a peculiar aesthetic of action and propaganda in trying to further spread his ideology. The ex-president's Sunday motorcycle tours through Brazilian cities, accompanied by his supporters, derived directly from the aesthetic of Benito Mussolini, who, as we know, appropriated the futurist cult of machines to instill in the social imaginary the ideal of a superior, virile

---

[30] S. Freud, *Der Mann Moses und die monotheistische Religion* (English translation: *Moses and Monotheism*), 1939, pp. 23-43.

white society. The Bolsonaro government has made clear its sympathy with this ideal, one of the keys to reinforcing European colonialism and Nazi-fascism.

Spreading such an ideal, of course, is a stealth operation! Bolsonarism borrowed Trump's strategy of "dog-whistle politics" to transmit its attraction to a certain target group (ultra-rightist champions of white supremacy). The codified language of the "dog whistle" is doubt: if, on the one hand, it appeals to the neo-Nazi groups and the racists who 'get' it, on the other hand, it goes undetected by those who can't hear its subliminal message of hatred of the other. When, in a live spot transmitted over YouTube, the president of the republic held up a cup of milk on the pretext of wanting to toast the dairy cooperatives, this racist gesture adopted by white supremacists made his ideological position quite clear. If caught out, he'd answer critics that he was being misinterpreted. One reading identified "dog-whistle politics" as one of the causes of the dizzying rise since the 2018 election of hitherto masked militants who adhere to neo-Nazi thinking, discourse, and aesthetics, in addition to others who declare themselves fascists, fundamentalists, or promoters of some sort of racist propaganda. The data were worrisome: it was estimated that there existed 536 neo-Nazi cells in Brazil. In 2019, there were 334, which pointed to a 58 percent rise, according to the daily *O Globo*.

Along these lines, violence against the human group that has suffered and continues to suffer the most racist attacks in Brazil-Blacks-shot up, whereas the rate of criminal mortality against white citizens declined. The government flatly denied this evidence. After the murder of a Black man, João Alberto Freitas, whom two white police officers strangled in a supermarket in Rio Grande do Sul, both the president and vice-president tried to deny the existence of racism in the country. Both appealed to the myth of Brazil as a "racial democracy" to negate this racist deed so reminiscent of George Floyd's murder in the U.S. in 2020.

Although the reality of recent Brazilian politics has been extremely worrying, one must acknowledge that the Bolsonarist language and aesthetic, for all that it mimicked the mass psychology implanted by the Third Reich, fit all too easily into another historical context and a different social space than that of the 1930s, into a civilization perhaps more "evolved" in many senses. Yet history has grown weary by now of showing that progress does not mean a guarantee against barbarism.

The gullibility of the Brazilian people to the watchwords and the incendiary actions of their nation's current leader clearly *also met with strong resistance*. The memory of the Brazilian people still functioned as a permanent archive to individual and social workings-out of collective trauma despite the government's efforts to deny and even foreclose the fundamental lesson in Brazil's recent political history—the military coup of 1964 and of AI-5.[31] It's an archive that blocked the president's intent to speak for the people and also served as resistance to any nostalgic idealization of the military dictatorship, to the snares of national identity and the manipulation of the unruly movement of the drives.

Post-Election Coda

In late October 2022, the incumbent Bolsonaro, despite having the State machine in his favor and a busily functioning system of disinformation (above all after the 2016 dispute that handed Donald Trump the presidency), lost to former president Luiz Inácio Lula da Silva, albeit by a very slender margin (49.1 to Lula's 50.9% of the vote). Pro-Bolsonaro demonstrators objecting to the results showed the same disdain for the law that Trump's followed did when Joe Biden was elected: they too denied election results through violent protests in public places. Truck and taxi drivers who were given government money handouts the night before the election occupied some of the country's main highways, blocking free movement and jeopardizing people's access to basic food supplies, medication, or medical care. Even two months after the election, many Bolsonaro loyalists continued to camp out in front of Army barracks, demanding military intervention, on the far-fetched claim that fraud had taken place in the vote count. Copying the assault on the Capitol in Washington, an attempt was made in Brazil's capital Brasilia to invade the Federal Police building.

The language and the aesthetic of the Third Reich were flaunted throughout the country. In Santa Catarina, one of the wealthiest

---

[31] Institutional Act Number Five was the fifth of seventeen major decrees issued by the military dictatorship in the years following the 1964 coup d'état in Brazil. *Institutional Acts* were the highest form of legislation during the military regime, since they overruled even the highly authoritarian Constitution, and were enforced without the possibility of judicial review. They were issued on behalf of the Supreme Command of the Revolution (the regime's leadership).

and most important states in Brazil, the participants in a protest gave the Nazi salute as the Brazilian flag was hoisted to the tune of the national anthem. This replica of a common scene in Germany and the countries the Third Reich conquered from the 1930s to the end of the Second World War found its echo in another unbelievable occurrence: a 16-year-old boy brandishing a swastika shot at students and teachers in a school.

"They tried to bury me alive and I'm still here," exclaimed Lula at the start of his speech the day of his election.[32] One can view this remark, of course, as a demagogue's ploy to steer his followers' hatred against their common enemy. Yet undeniably Brazil at large has recently suffered numerous attempts to be "buried," choked by fires deliberately set to its forests, by ethnocide of its indigenous peoples, extermination of Black citizens, and the dizzying social inequality starving many thousands of Brazilians. But can the returned leader identified with the pariahs, the foreign-and-alien of Brazil, avoid falling in turn into the trap of a totalitarian discourse denying the differences of his large opposition? Must social inclusiveness remain impossible?[33]

By way of the democratic vote Brazil seems to have survived the dark times. Yet the damage caused by the spread of hate speech to all four corners of the country cannot be overestimated. This is a fact of fundamental importance for understanding the growing "outbursts of violence" in large segments of society, from the lower to the more affluent class. Here we must include the destruction of public health

---

[32] In 2017, Sérgio Mouro, then a federal judge, sentenced Lula to nine years and six months in prison for the crimes of passive corruption and money laundering. Later the sentence was increased to twelve years and one month. In August 2018, the UN Human Rights Committee asked Brazil to guarantee Lula exercise of his political rights while in prison, including access to his party members and the media and participation in the presidential election in Brazil in 2018. The Ministry of Foreign Affairs of Brazil questioned the Committee and forwarded the decision to the Judiciary. In 2021, the Supreme Court annulled Lula's convictions, and with that he regained his political rights. On April 28, 2022, the UN Human Rights Committee published its conclusion in an analysis pointing out that Sergio Moro had shown partiality in his judgment of the cases against Lula. According to the Committee's decision, the accused had his political rights violated in 2018 after being kept from participating in the year's presidential elections and determined that Brazil should present the measures adopted to repair damages caused to the former president within 180 days, and to prevent other people from being the target of similar processes in the future.

[33] Y. Stavrakakis, *Lacan y lo Político*, Prometeo Libros, Buenos Aires, pp. 186-191.

policies and the cultural wreckage resulting from the horde tasked with glorifying the idea of absolute power. It should be pointed out, then, that the violence taking root in the country over recent years has gone beyond its purpose to forge social links that could restore a more heterogeneous society.

During the First World War Freud noticed that after going through a long period of mourning for what we have lost "it will be found that our high opinion of the riches of civilization has lost nothing from our discovery of their fragility. We shall build up again all that war has destroyed, and perhaps on firmer ground and more lastingly than before."[34] We Brazilians "shall build up again all that Bolsonarism has destroyed." But we must be careful not to succumb to the temptation of hiding the political divisions in our society and so denying difference. As Alain Touraine pointed out,[35] ensuring social integration means respecting the social forces, the interests and opinions that have rightly operated in the social realm, which is very different from the ideological strategy of denying the constitutive divisions at the heart of society.

In light of Freud's text on the transience of life and things, we must recognize that the task of the psychoanalyst, beyond one-on-one clinical practice, is to serve as critic of the destructive movements that invade and threaten civilization, whatever they may be, independent of the ideological field in which they're inserted. An arduous task, since in the current moment, such movements are being promoted by leaders elected by the people (as Hitler was), and who, in occupying their offices, take and occlude the place formerly occupied by the dead father—the place of the void, the empty place that impels the evolution of democracy.[36]

(Translated by David Jacobson)

---

[34] S. Freud, "On Transience," in *Complete Psychological Works, op. cit.*, Vol. XIV (1916), p. 307.

[35] A. Touraine, "What does democracy mean today?" in *International Social Sciences Journal* 128, 1991, p. 261.

[36] C. Lefort, *A invenção democrática*, Editora Brasiliense, São Paulo, 1981 [*L'Invention démocratique. Les limites de la domination totalitaire*]. Influenced by psychoanalysis, Lefort upholds the idea that no empirical agent belongs naturally in the empty place of power. For the maintenance of the democratic order and that of the State, the place of the dead Father can never be occupied, lest it hinder the emergence of conflicts and dichotomies that allow the very movement of democracy to occur.

Obsessional Neurosis: An Allegory of Our Time
Alain Vanier

The clinical categories with which we think about our practices are profoundly linked to the era in which they arise. Ian Hacking has shown this remarkably, in charting the emergence of the notion of the "pathological voyage" at the end of the 19th century, i.e. at the very moment mass tourism was developing.[1] Which is not to say that vagrancy of this sort didn't previously exist. The same question can be posed for all classifications, which by no means robs them of interest; it simply leads to questioning them. From this perspective we can ask why obsessional neurosis—identified by Freud at the birth of psychoanalysis—was isolated only at the end of the 19th century.

The Emergence of Obsessional Neurosis

The term obsession, in the sense we use it today, is recent, at least in French. Only at the end of the 18th century (1799, to be precise) does it come to mean an image or an idea that haunts us. Before the mid-19th century the very word was still rare, largely confined to medical language. Ostensibly, Jules Falret introduced it into psychiatry. Krafft-Ebing speaks of compulsion, *Zwangsvorstellung*, to denote some unbidden representation impressed upon the mind. But the first description that gives it the status of a clinical type was offered by Legrand du Saulle in 1875, in a text entitled "Madness of doubt (with delirium of touch)."[2] He considers it a madness of consciousness, or, to be more precise, a "pathology of intelligence," and he assigns it three consecutive stages. First, "the spontaneous, involuntary and irresistible production of certain sequences of thoughts

---

[1] I. Hacking, *Mad Travelers: Reflections on the Reality of Transient Mental Illnesses*, Harvard University Press, Cambridge, MA, 2002.

[2] H. Legrand du Saulle, *La Folie du doute (avec délire du toucher)*, Adrien Delahaye, Paris, 1875.

on undetermined, theoretical, abstract, or ridiculous subjects, free of illusion and sensory hallucinations." During this period, the struggle is a silent one: persons under siege do not complain of what is besieging them. Next come "unexpected revelations to family, friends, and those around him." Noted too is the appearance of "exaggerated scruples; wildly fanciful fears; anxieties and misgivings; thoughts of suicide and occasional attempts at voluntary death." But also, veritable fits of excitement, with preliminary epigastric aura; aversion to some animals, as well as a considerable lessening of doubt and of personal questionings. The subject also needs to harp on the same matters to the same person in order to be constantly reassured by them in identical, and if possible preestablished, terms. It is in this stage that the fear of touching certain objects arises, hence repeated washing and various eccentricities. The subject readily admits to these excessive acts. Legrand du Saulle emphasizes: "always with fully maintained intelligence." At this stage, haunting thoughts are dealt with through rituals that often involve someone else. Ultimately, the situation becomes intolerable for subjects, all sociability tends to vanish, the normal acts of life are impossible, it becomes quite hard for them to go outside; movements slow down and several hours are expended on morning grooming or on each of the day's meals. The circle of "delirious" ideas shrinks and anxiety increases proportionally, yet dementia never comes. "These strange and unfortunate sick people have the most absolute awareness of their state." Some find relief through a great effort of will and substitute reasonable ideas for the one that assails them, by performing philanthropic, religious or patriotic acts.

Freud alludes to "madness of doubt" in 1894 in his paper "Obsessions and Phobias," then brings obsessional neurosis into being in "Heredity and the Aetiology of the Neuroses" in 1896.[3] Both articles were written in French, and he used the French term *obsession* together with the German *Zwangsneurose* (neurosis of compulsion):

> I was obliged to begin my work with a nosographic innovation. I found reason to set alongside of hysteria the obsessional neurosis (*Zwangsneurose*) as a self-sufficient and independent disorder. [...] The obsessional

---

[3] S. Freud, "Obsessions and Phobias" (1895*c* [1894]). and "Heredity and the Aetiology of the Neuroses" (1896*a*), in *The Standard Edition of the Complete Psychological Works of Sigmund Freud*, Vol. III, trans. J. Strachey, The Hogarth Press, London, 1962.

neurosis (*Zwangsneurose*) arises from a specific cause very analogous to that of hysteria. Here too we find a precocious sexual event, occurring before puberty, the memory of which becomes active during or after that period; and the same remarks and arguments which I put forward in connection with hysteria will apply to my observations of the other neurosis (six cases, three of which were pure ones). There is only one difference which seems capital. At the basis of the aetiology of hysteria we found an event of passive sexuality, an experience submitted to with indifference or with a small degree of annoyance or fright. In obsessional neurosis it is a question on the other hand, of an event which has given pleasure, of an act of aggression inspired by desire (in the case of a boy) or of a participation in sexual relations accompanied by enjoyment (in the case of a little girl). The obsessional ideas, when their intimate meaning has been recognized by analysis, when they have been reduced, as it were, to their simplest expression, are nothing other than reproaches addressed by the subject himself on account of this anticipated sexual enjoyment, but reproaches distorted by an unconscious psychical work of transformation and substitution.[4]

A traumatic encounter has occurred, and jouissance has been tied to a feeling of guilt: if Freud discovers psychoanalysis with hysterics, he also isolates obsessional neurosis, later claiming it is the neurosis of defense he knows best. He will stress that due to the sheer clinical multiplicity of obsessional neurosis, any coherent synthesis of all its variations will always fall short. Lacan too will insist on how variably it presents itself.

Obsessional neurosis is thus Freud's contribution to the "clinic of the past;" yet, it seems emblematic of the time we're living in. This is not to say that we're all becoming obsessionals, but that the existence of this neurosis gives a particular character to our time.

The Clinic of Obsessional Neurosis[5]

Obsessional neurosis is the finding of a forbidden jouissance, repressed but fixed, which thought tries in vain to process. It's an illness

---

[4] S. Freud, "Heredity," *op. cit.*, pp. 146, 155.

[5] See A. Vanier, "Aujourd'hui, la névrose obsessionnelle," *L'Évolution psychiatrique*, 70 (1), Elsevier, Janvier-Mars 2005; and A. Vanier, "Névrose obsessionnelle, névrose idéale," *Figures de la psychanalyse* 12, érès, Ramonville Saint-Agne, 2006.

of thought, "a thought that troubles the soul, which does not know what to do with it."[6] Unlike hysteria, in obsessional neurosis there is no mechanism of repression that grounds forgetting, but rather a disjunction of causal relation and a displacement of affect. These deformations serve to mask some primal reproach.

One might also define obsessional neurosis as an illness that relates to separation, insofar as alienation to the signifier suspends the question of the obsessional's desire.[7] Obsessionals, more than anyone else, experience dependence on the desire of the Other. Whence their subjective clinging in their confrontation with an Other already dead but who must, at the same time, be killed. A strange formula, this "killing the father," since the father is always already dead, and obsessionals, in their wish to kill him, never cease to assert that he's still alive. It's impossible for obsessionals to desire, since desire, if it is possible, implies the destruction of the Other they need as a guarantee: they are constantly in the process of negating, undoing, this Other, while preserving it—which explains the ceaseless oscillation their hopeless doubt generates.

More than other neuroses, obsessional neurosis reveals the contemporary paradox of the father. The obsessional's father is inadequate, a father at fault, which prompts a certain failure of the paternal metaphor. That metaphor, though, is what allows for a separation, for a loss of objects, thanks to the sexual meaning assumed by the objects during the developmental stages. Obsessionals turn, therefore, to the figure of the imaginary father as a figure of mastery. But this leads to an impasse. In constructing this figure they attempt, at the same time, to cancel it, to murder the father. This is the paradox described by *Totem and Taboo*, which Lacan considered the obsessional myth par excellence. But murdering the father in no way annuls his command-

---

[6] J. Lacan "Télévision" (1973-74), in *Autres Écrits*, Éditions du Seuil, Paris, 2001, p. 512.

[7] According to Lacan, alienation and separation are the two operations in the causation of the subject. See J. Lacan, *The Four Fundamental Concepts of Psychoanalysis*, Seminar XI, Norton & Company, London & New York, 1978, Chapters 16 and 17. "Alienation resides in the subject's division," J. Lacan, 1966. "Position of the Unconscious," in *Écrits*, trans. Bruce Fink, Norton, New York, 2006, p. 708, since the signifier represents the subject for another signifier. Separation follows "the subject's causation" in its dialectic relation to the Other. The subject questions what is not being said in the discourse of the Other, those blanks in discourse where the subject posits "its own lack" (*Ibid.*, English, p. 716).

ments—which is why Freud viewed obsessional neurosis as an effect of angst in the face of the superego.

The father of the Rat Man senses this murderous dimension after his little boy, in his rage, calls him "a lamp," "a napkin," and so on.[8] Lacan regards these insults as a radical metaphor. We must give up the cliché that depicts the obsessional as some sort of compliant hack or civil servant. A colleague was called upon to assess one of the major criminals of the last few decades; after meeting him, he told me how surprised he was to have to diagnose him as an obsessional neurotic. The lethal relation to the father reflects the obsessional sense of guilt and the demand for love the son addresses to him in order to undo his hatred. But this also accounts for his inhibition, since his love for the father also feminizes him.

The obsessional problematic brings about a particular relation to jouissance, one that obsessionals hang onto and capitalize upon. In fact, they're vying less with the father than with the imaginary phallus under the gaze of the Other. This Other is conceived as deriving its enjoyment by looking at them while stripping them of their jouissance.[9] Under the constant gaze of the Other, they engage in daring exploits. However solitary these acts may be, they are always addressed to the Other's gaze.

The dominant defense mechanism in obsessional neurosis is displacement, unlike hysteria, which is ruled by repression. Freud, however, referred to obsessional neurosis as a dialect of hysteria, and insisted there is always a hysterical underpinning to every case of obsessional neurosis, a position Lacan would share at the end of his teaching. One can even add that manifestation of hysteria in the obsessional's treatment is a sign of progress. Also, Freud thought that an obsessional neurosis could turn into paranoia.

Whereas hysterics work out a compromise between contradictory tendencies and give in to an erotic satisfaction through their symptoms, obsessionals distance, or circumvent, that satisfaction. For an obsessional, instead of compromise, there are two opposite tendencies that follow on each other, ushering in a hopeless, dead-end jouissance. This jouissance emerges in destructive outbursts, in

---

[8] S. Freud, *Notes upon a Case of Obsessional Neurosis* (1909), *Standard Edition, op. cit.*, Vol. X, p. 205.

[9] S. Faladé, *Clinique des névroses*, Anthropos Economica, Paris, 2003.

fastidiousness, in those child's tantrums so poorly tolerated by the parents who feel utterly negated by them, or for that matter, in the hyperkinesis of those children treated today by all sorts of medications. One ritual replaces another. The defensive outcome consists, then, of rituals, various ceremonies, but also of the working out of a strategy toward desire that replaces it with the demand of the Other. Thus, in every relation with a partner, including the analyst, "it is their desire that hysterical demand interests; that it is his or her demand that the obsessional's desire wants to bring out at any cost."[10] For obsessionals, as for hysterics, desire is desire of the Other; but hysterics, in some sense, know this and may even be questing after it, whereas obsessionals want to know nothing about it, since they experience this desire as a contamination. They need to deny the desire of the Other, since the real of the Other's jouissance is too close for comfort and the impossibility of erasing oneself as a subject isn't just a concern for mastery or vigilance, but above all, to prevent being confused with the object one might become for the jouissance of this Other.

What obsessionals attempt to think about is literally unthinkable, since it is Real: "the Real [. . .] can be thought about only as impossible. That is to say, whenever it rears its head, it's unthinkable. It would be hopeless to approach this impossibility, since this unthinkable is death, it is the foundation of the Real that death cannot be thought."[11] This is the dead-end obsessionals confront, though it's also their tireless quest: to master the Real through thought, and thereby annul it. Death, for them, is one of the names for castration.

In hysteria, as the Oedipus myth illustrates, desire is unsatisfied because the law is original, preceding the crime: the mother is desired because she is forbidden. In *Totem and Taboo*, the law follows the unlimited jouissance of the father of the horde. The superego emerges here in an appeal: *Jouis*, You must enjoy! In a certain sense, this gives

---

[10] J. Lacan:"[C]'est son désir que la demande hystérique intéresse; que c'est sa demande que le désir de l'obsessionnel veut faire surgir à tout prix." Interview by François Wahl on the publication of Écrits, radio broadcast of February 8, 1967. *Bulletin de l'Association freudienne* 3, Paris, 1983.

[11] J. Lacan, *Le sinthome, Le séminaire Livre XXIII*, Éditions du Seuil, Paris, 2005, p. 125: "le réel [...] ne peut être pensé que comme impossible. C'est-à-dire que chaque fois qu'il montre le bout de son nez, il est impensable. Aborder cet impossible ne saurait constituer un espoir, puisque cet impensable, c'est la mort, dont c'est le fondement du réel qu'elle ne puisse être pensée."

it an imaginary consistency. Freud's dream, in Lacan's view, is that of the law of the father, which is why he posits the father's jouissance at the outset, implying his necessary murder. Obsessional desire clings to something impossible: the brothers will forbid themselves the women, at which point, nothing is possible anymore. The social pact implies the taboo on women, and is founded on the brothers' homosexuality and phallic rivalry.

So we come to understand the stakes behind the murder of the father, for his death screens out castration, leaving the hope that out of this will arise the missing signifier, for instance, as foundation for a religion. Since obsessionals can't relinquish their initial jouissance, they remain fixated on its alienating moment, which can never be expunged. Alienation implies that the subject is subjected to the signifier and has found itself shunted from one signifier to another; it seeks to reduce this interval in order to undo the irreducible gap and the Real to which it bears witness, tirelessly searching for the ultimate signifier to attain the last word, the last meaning. Otherwise, the founding signifying difference (as illustrated by the play of *fort-da* in *Beyond the Pleasure Principle*) remains irreducible and breeds non-sense. Obsessionals want to understand everything in order to annul the enigmatic dimension of the desire of the Other. And so they give, even before anything is demanded of them, and devote themselves to satisfying that demand in order to crush the desire of the Other, which is experienced as a commandment.

To be a subject divided by two signifiers is, for some, an unbearable condition. The malady of consciousness is a refusal of the unconscious. Which explains isolation rather than repression, since obsessionals can't be abolished as subjects, as their egoic clinging makes clear. "The obsessional (...) denies the desire of the Other in shaping his phantasm to accentuate the impossibility of the subject's disappearance."[12] Isolation masquerades as separation (washing one's hands, fearing germs, etcetera, in order not to be contaminated by the desire of the Other). It is an illusory separation to undo alienation.

---

[12] J. Lacan, "Subversion du sujet et dialectique du désir," in *Écrits*, Éditions du Seuil, Paris, 1966, p. 824: "L'obsessionnel (...) nie le désir de l'Autre en formant son fantasme à accentuer l'impossible de l'évanouissement du sujet." "The Subversion of the Subject and the Dialectic of Desire," in *Écrits: The First Complete Edition in English*, trans. Bruce Fink, *op. cit.*, p. 698.

Obsessionals try, then, to pay off an imaginary debt that links them to the Other, to whose language they remain attached. This is why these great rationalizers are fundamentally psychologists: Lacan could even say, "Who is more of a psychologist than an obsessional? He does psychology all day long. It's one of the forms of his illness."[13]

The Delusion of Autonomy

Clinically, we observe that transposing the initial commandment of the superego into thoughts, cut off from affects, prompts a surge of obsession-inducing speculations and absurd commandments, which are as such just so many displacements from their original cause. The obsessional neurotic is a thinker, a compulsive thinker who wants to owe nothing to the Other: "I can't think of nothing," one analysand would say. In this sense the obsessional incarnates the delusion of autonomy that Lacan considered characteristic of our era: being autonomous as an ideal, as an individual without the Other.

Lacan first brings up autonomy in his critique of the autonomous ego promoted by Hartmann, Kris, and Loewenstein, against which he begins his teaching.[14] But gradually he links the autonomous ego with what he calls a secret discourse, that of freedom, an unspoken message of liberation stifled by the fact of widespread voluntary servitude. In his seminar on the psychoses, Lacan comments: "We live in a society in which slavery isn't recognized. It's nevertheless clear (...) that it has in no way been abolished."[15] The plight of master-slave bondage lives in each of us with the discourse of freedom as its correlative. The individual's right to autonomy is the hallmark of modern man—and it is a delusional discourse.[16] What are the stakes of this delusion? Autonomy presupposes attaining a "completing object," the object that fills all lack. It is modern man's illusion to want to free himself from any quest for the object *while still finding such an object*, thereby eluding

---

[13] J. Lacan, "Discours de Tokyo," unpublished, 1971. "Quoi de plus psychologue qu'un obsessionel? Il fait de la psychologie a longueur de journée. C'est une des formes de sa maladie."

[14] J. Lacan, *Le Moi dans la théorie de Freud et dans la technique de la psychanalyse, Le séminaire Livre II* (1954-55), Éditions du Seuil, Paris, 1978, p. 20.

[15] J. Lacan, *Les Psychoses, Le séminaire Livre III* (1955-56), Éditions du Seuil, Paris, 1981, pp. 149-150.

[16] *Ibid.*, pp. 150-151.

all subjective conflict, all division. The wager is to free oneself from the encroachment of "manufactured objects": it's a matter of freeing oneself from the exacerbation of the promise that modern capitalism constitutes, freeing oneself from those gadgets that saturate desire; and yet, one never stops consuming all objects, in order to find the "completing" one. The "autonomous self" leads to behaviorism, right up to its latest version: full mindfulness, personal development, New Age yoga, the perfect diet, self-healing, etc., all practices that promise freedom and autonomy. The obsessional, as psychologist, is the champion of Selfhood as the promise of freedom and autonomy.

Yet the autonomy of the ego "is never so manifest as when it is serving another's law, being subjected to that law in the very act of defending against it, by first misrecognizing it."[17] In this framework, being an object for the Other produces angst—an angst that is counter-phobically covered by the Ideal-Ego image of autonomy.

As Winnicott pointed out, such angst is masked by the proliferation of objects. The autonomy of the ego is a return to the discourse of the Master, to the mastery of the ego, a twist of the capitalist's discourse to reestablish the master's discourse. This is what is at stake in this autonomy: to free oneself from objects in reestablishing a Master's discourse that feeds a pompous Ego, whose illusory autonomy goes hand in hand with the mirroring image of the other and masks one's voluntary servitude. It's not by chance that today we're witnessing pretty much everywhere a call for new masters.

Thought and Drive

The theoretical-clinical approach to obsessional neurosis is paradoxical. It is risky for us to approach it on its own terms, through its own means, since obsessional neurotics are thinkers; or rather, they *are* thought, cogitation. Obsessional neurosis involves an eroticization of thought, an incessant return of the link between jouissance and the signifier. The true unit of measurement for obsessional neurotics is the imaginary phallus, and, in their formulations, there is always

---

[17] J. Lacan, "Remarque sur le rapport de Daniel Lagache: Psychanalyse et structure de la personnalité" (1960), in *Écrits*, Éditions du Seuil, Paris, 1966, p. 668: "cette autonomie du moi] ne se manifeste jamais tant qu'à servir la loi d'un autre en la subissant de s'en défendre, à partir de la méconnaître."

an equivalence that brings in a phallic value. What this shows is that thought is a parasite that affects the body. "Thought is not a category. I'm tempted to say it's an affect. One might even say that it's the most fundamental thing from the standpoint of affect."[18]   For the obsessional's thoughts are the effect of affects on the body, the effect of the engagement of the body in discourse. They're not outside discourse, since the obsessional derives jouissance from them.

Two drives are at stake here: the drive of looking and knowing, as Freud points out, and the anal drive, two drives that put into play an object. The anal object is subjectified by the Other's demand. The caretaker demand orders the child both to retain and to give—an obsessional conundrum. The object takes on the value of a body part. Yet the demand, as a gift, is ambiguous, since this object, though gazed on and admired, is immediately thrown away. Passage to the phallic level won't mitigate this position: this object—feces, excrement—wonderfully symbolises and embodies the phallus: there one moment and gone the next, it appears, then disappears. Faced with the impossibility of being satisified at the phallic level, the anal object will come to serve as a stopper; it illustrates the loss of the phallus. The anal level will recover the real of non-relation, and the anal object keeps the subject on the edge of the hole of castration. It is an anal dimension that comes to represent the subject. In turn, the genital act assumes the form of a gift. The other side of shit, of course, is idealization. At the level of demand, the anal bond seems to symbolize everything. Yet there remains desire, necessary if one is not to be reduced to the object of the demand. In France we say of someone with a high self-regard, 'Il ne se prend pas pour de la merde,' one doesn't treat oneself like shit; but indeed, what one fears here is being the object that needs to be dropped.[19] The anal act implies motor mastery; the narcissistic medium of self-mastery passes through a mirror image, a medium in which the object is detached, all the more since it comes from a part of the body that the subject doesn't see.

---

[18] J. Lacan, *L'envers de la psychanalyse, Le séminaire Livre XVII*, Éditions du Seuil, Paris, 1991, p. 176.

[19] The scopic dimension is articulated here, as Lacan indicated. He connects anal and scopic drives in his diagram of the object in his seminar of 1962-63 on Angst, in the session of June 19, 1963, Paris, Édition du Seuil, 2004, p. 358.

Obsessional neurosis is inherent to consciousness, but it's a consciousness of spectacle that divides into two, between the position of the actor and that of the viewer, a doubling up that takes stock of these constant oscillations. The scopic level, Lacan emphasizes, is the one that best masks castration. Idealization is the correlative of this level of the drive. The ideal is imagined as a god, as the controlling eye, observing all our actions.

A Contemporary Economy of Jouissance

For Freud, "an obsessional neurosis presents a travesty, half comic and half tragic, of a private religion."[20] If religion is humanity's universal obsessional neurosis, and if accepting the universal neurosis relieves true believers of the task of fashioning themselves a personal religion,[21] then obsessional neurosis can appear only on condition that religion is weakening and tradition is breaking apart as a manifest effect of the advance of the discourse of science, the progressive triumph of reason. Obsessional neurosis was isolated by Freud in a century in which religious doubt had taken broad hold, as Christopher Lane has masterfully shown in his work on Victorian literature.[22] Isn't this evidence of the diffraction of traditional religious belief into so many private religions? In this setting, *Totem and Taboo* takes its rightful place as the clinical myth of our time.

Lacan saw in obsessional neurosis a way out of the struggle of master and slave that didn't occur to Hegel—not without historical reason, perhaps. The slave would play dead, in anticipatory identification with the awaited death of the master. S/he waits, which is why s/he procrastinates endlessly. This is also why obsessionals can sometimes experience a sense of relief upon the real death of their parents: only now can they begin to live. Slaves attempt to fool their masters by showing their good will, thereby trying to mitigate the aggressive intention that keeps them bound to the Other. This reality is not unrelated to the recent efforts to inflate the value of work in our world.

---

[20] S. Freud, "Obsessive Actions and Religious Practices" (1907), *Standard Edition, op. cit.*, Vol. IX, p. 119.

[21] S. Freud, *The Future of an Illusion* (1927), *Standard Edition*, Vol. XXI.

[22] C. Lane, *The Age of Doubt: Tracing the Roots of Our Religious Uncertainty*, Yale University Press, New Haven, 2011.

It is here that obsessionals give evidence of their modernity, not merely through their asociality, their penchant for isolation in these times of loneliness, but also through their subjection to petty leaders, transitional ideal fathers. Such allegiances grant them a certain mobility, a rekindling of the quest for a father who knows something about his desire and his jouissance. This is a quest for meaning and for the ultimate signifier, which explains the obsessional's fascination for those who know something about jouissance. As Lacan points out, in their quest for meaning obsessionals try to reach an origin, the time of the sign that precedes the signifying articulation. We're not done with religion, however frail it became over the last century. Its return, as heralded by Lacan, pervades discourse, for instance, in the role love assumes in the parental bond, or in the frightful unveiling of the link between religion and jouissance and all its spectacular performances. Yet when religion returns, it's not necessarily to the same place. It is important to note that obsessionals aren't necessarily fixated on the "you must be like your father," and what that implies; they may also be fixated, in a thoroughly sterile way, on "you mustn't be like father." Either way, the erection of an imaginary father to whom they subject themselves or against whom they rebel is a necessity.

But far from their lack of satisfaction finding accommodations in the insatiable production of the lack of jouissance, they call for gadgetry to provide satisfaction in order to limit the rise of excitation, ever in search of the next object that will ensure the phallicity of their being under the Other's gaze. Thus, the figure of the obsessional as metaphysician is partially replaced by the obsessional as collector, a collector of everything, from the relics of an imaginary father to matchboxes, not to mention women or men. But this quest is oriented by the search for a "completing object" that, even if it were found, would have to be destroyed, annihilated. Such a search is guided by the hope of finding a sign from the Other who could absolve them of their guilt.

In this way they undo separation, momentarily transforming an object of exchange into a non-exchangeable object. If obsessionals seek to unify and erase the gap between the first signifiers, a gap that produces the object, it is, paradoxically, this object that they collect. The imaginary phallus, the unit of measurement for their entire libidinal economy, introduces into their world an equivalence of all metonymic objects which allows for undoing the division of the signifier. They hope such objects are retrievable. These considerations reflect

Lacan's writing of the matheme of the capitalist discourse. Consider the Rat Man and the equivalence he sets up between rats and money. The inversion of the places and letters of the first part of the discourse of the Master in the capitalist discourse makes it impossible to tell who the master is in modern mastery.[23] The lost object is placed directly in relation to the subject, an object for plugging up its division and canceling the difference inherent in signifiers.[24] In keeping with the secularization of the promise to recover a lost jouissance, jouissance is possible no longer when death is near, as religions preach, but right here on Earth, in the form of consumption. Understandably, then, where hysterics look for the desire of the Other to find their bearings, obsessionals are oriented by the object, the *plus-de-jouir*, the extra jouissance at play in demand. This orientation is precarious, mere surplus-value, from which obsessionals are exonerated by heeding the call to do-gooder deeds.[25] Quite the modern economy of jouissance!

Obsessionals' refusal of the unconscious expresses itself in the ideal of transparency and mastery, an Enlightenment ideal, a dream of the triumph of Reason, whence their interest in the psychologies of consciousness. The moment something starts to shift in their treatment, obsessionals may suddenly start devouring books of psychoanalysis—if they haven't done so before their first analytic session.

Hysteria bore witness to the capture of the body by the scientific medicine of the end of the 19th century, a sharp turn that misrecognized desire and jouissance in the body, consigning them to industrial production. In manifesting thought as an illness, obsessional neurosis bore witness to the new world of information, of accumulation of knowledge, big data, of the proliferation of discourses, the annexation of thought by technics, with storage of considerable memories in the "clouds" and the net bulging with answers in the face of gaps in knowledge—all of which are founded on the sidelining of the link between signifier and jouissance.

---

[23]
$$\downarrow \frac{S}{S_1} \times \frac{S_2}{a} \downarrow \qquad \uparrow \frac{S_1 \to S_2}{S \times a} \downarrow$$

[24] J. Lacan "Du discours psychanalytique," in *Lacan in Italia 1953-1978*, La Salamandra, Milan, 1978.

[25] J. Lacan, *On the Summons to Philanthropic Activity* (*l'humanitairerie de commande*), see "Télévision," in *Autres Écrits*, Paris, Seuil, 1973, p. 534.

In obsessional neurosis the jouissance one wants to eliminate returns: just think of the current "cleansing" operations politically correct expression tries to carry out against various objectionable terms and intentions. It is a memorial of *lalangue* in this world in which language is reduced to communication, as Walter Benjamin put it.

In 1978, Lacan ended the congress of the École freudienne de Paris with the following affirmation: "Neuroses exist. By this I mean that it's not very certain that hysterical neurosis still exists, but there is surely one neurosis that exists, it's what is called obsessional neurosis."[26] Six years earlier he could claim that obsessional neurosis finds "no place in any discourse that holds,"[27] and, in fact, in his Seminar *The Other Side of Psychoanalysis*, he articulated four discourses, one of them being the discourse of the hysteric, a social link that finds a secure basis in its relation to the new figures of mastery. Obsessional neurosis embodies quite well the figure of consumer modernity, of the solitary jouissance enabled by technical advances, with everyone glutted and overwhelmed by gadgets, all those objects Hannah Arendt noted were produced only in order to be destroyed.[28] In fact, this perspective of destruction may be precisely what gives them value in the eyes of certain people. Obsessional neurosis is an allegory of our time, in Walter Benjamin's sense of the term: "Allegories are in the realm of thought what ruins are in the realm of things."[29] Obsessionals are the vestige of a vanishing world. They embody the subject's resistance to its "objectalization," bent on the uniqueness and singleness of the self. This is why obsessional neurosis is currently in full evidence, while hysteria has taken on a lower profile, absorbed by the world of the technosciences. Hysteria may be more discreet due to the existence of what Lacan called "psychoanalytic looniness,"[30] but above all, thanks

---

[26] J. Lacan, Conclusions du *9ᵉ Congrès de l'École Freudienne de Paris sur "La transmission," op. cit.*: "Les névroses, *ça* existe. Je veux dire qu'il n'est pas très sûr que la névrose hystérique existe toujours, mais il y a sûrement une névrose qui existe, c'est ce qu'on appelle la névrose obsessionnelle."

[27] "...De ne trouver place dans aucun discours qui tienne." J. Lacan, "Du discours psychanalytique," *op. cit.*

[28] H. Arendt *Condition de l'homme moderne*, trans. G. Fradier, Calmann-Lévy, Paris, 1961.

[29] W. Benjamin, *Origine du drame baroque allemand*, trans. S. Muller (with A. Hirt), Flammarion, Paris, 1985, p. 191.

[30] Lacan's term is "loufoquerie psychanalytique," and he wonders if such "looniness"

to the exploitation of desire. Industrializing desire is the best way to calm people down. Lack of satisfaction is basic, yet today we're no longer in the register of general discontent: quite the contrary, we're saturated with wished for objects.

In the overall management of dissatisfaction by a disciplinary law, haven't we entered, as Deleuze pointed out, the society of control, where "one's never done with anything"?[31] The "apparent acquittal" procedures of disciplinary societies described by Foucault, which took upon themselves the treatment for error and guilt, have given way to "*unlimited procrastination (l'atermoiement illimité)* in the societies of control," in which "man is no longer locked-in man but indebted man," indebted to a diffused law, a law one can never be quits with, as obsessional neurosis so unremittingly shows.

(*Translated by David Jacobson*)

---

may have replaced the hysterical symptoms and neuroses of the past in "Propos sur l'hystérie" (1977), ed. Jacques-Alain Miller, *Quarto* 90, juin 2007.

[31] G. Deleuze, "Post-scriptum sur les sociétés de contrôle," in *Pourparlers*, Éditions de Minuit, Paris, 1990, p. 243.

Pitfalls: Notes on Love's Servitude[1]
Paola Mieli

> "But to fall in love does not mean to love. You can fall in love, while hating."
> Dostoyevsky, *The Brothers Karamazov*

On January 6, 2021, an excited and violent crowd assaulted the National Capitol in Washington D.C. with the goal of overturning the results of the Presidential election. Donald Trump addressed it in these terms:

"We love you... You are very special."

As extravagant, unthinkable, and astonishing as the scene might appear at the very heart of American democracy, the banal and, in their immediacy, transparent words of the legitimately defeated leader belong to a long history of manipulation of the masses, of tyrannies and enslavements. It isn't by chance that Freud, when he addresses the question of the nature of the mass, about which so much has been written and so much remains to say, shifts the interpretative axis onto the notion of love. Rereading today, once more, *Massenpsychologie und Ich-Analyse*,[2] one can only be troubled by its pertinence, even if some of its observations may seem remote to us. At a distance of one hundred years, in a different political and historical climate, one can only be struck by the analogies—including the fact of having found ourselves in a devastating pandemic and, perhaps, still inscribed in an era inaugurated, in the West and the Middle East, by the political and geographic consequences of the First World War. The enigma of the

---

[1] Published in "Trampas. Notas sobre la esclavitud del amor," in Pavón-Cuéllar, David; Fuks, Betty; Mieli, Paola, coords, *Más allá de la psicología social: Freud, las masas y el análisis del yo*, Paradiso Editores, México, D.F., 2023.

[2] In English the title reads *Group Psychology and the Analysis of the Ego*, engendering a confusion between the notion of "mass", or "crowd", and the notion of "group", which, in Freud's thinking, are not commensurate.

fascination for the leader, of the nature of totalitarianism inspired by the universal or that of voluntary servitude which is its corollary, are today just as enduring. And the examples are many.

After his fundamental writings on metapsychology, launched by *The Introduction to Narcissism*, in *Massenpsychologie* Freud feels the need to return to his definition of the libido and give it the most complete explanation, as "the energy of the drives related to everything that can be summarized by the word love,"[3] which, according to him, coincides with Plato's Eros, and the "love above all things" celebrated by the Apostle Paul in his Letter to the Corinthians.

Freud tries to give an answer to a question that had traversed the history of modern political philosophy, masterfully expressed by La Boétie in his *Discourse on Voluntary Servitude*.[4] La Boétie uses the terms "fascination," "bewitchment," "love," to describe the force that cements constraint and servitude "in the name of One"—and it is this force and the power of One that Freud treats in this text.

Freud notes that when sociologists and psychologists study the nature of the individual in the mass, the influence that the mass exerts over the individual's life and over the annulment of various drive inhibitions, they invariably have recourse to the magical word 'suggestion', or to something subsumed to it—imitation, empathy, contagion, and so on—turning it into a primary phenomenon of the human psyche. It was precisely the study of the phenomenon of suggestion that initiated a new understanding of psychic phenomena and opened the way for the invention of psychoanalysis. To the tyranny of suggestion such as he had seen it at work in Bernheim's theater of hysteria, Freud replies with the theory of drives, examining its aspects, articulating the

---

[3] S. Freud, *Massenpsychologie und Ich-Analyse*, Gesammelte Werke XIII, S. Fischer Verlag, Frankfurt, 1987, pp. 98-99.

[4] "…understand how it can be that so many men, so many towns, so many cities, so many nations, sometimes accept a tyrant who has only the power they give him, who only has the power to harm them to the extent they are willing to endure it, and who could not harm them in the least if they didn't prefer putting up with anything from him to contradicting him. This is such an amazing thing—and yet so common that it is better to greet it with sorrow than astonishment—to see a million men miserably enslaved, yoked, not because they are constrained by force, but because they are fascinated and so to speak, bewitched by the name alone of one they shouldn't fear, since he is alone, nor should they love, since he is inhuman." E. de La Boétie, *Le discours de la servitude volontaire*, text established by Pierre Léonard, Editions Payot, Paris, 1976, pp. 194-195.

concepts of narcissism, identification, enamoration, Ego ideal, as well as the different positions the object occupies relative to the Ego. If the autoerotic drives are absolutely primordial, there does not exist at the beginning a unit comparable to the Ego: *das Ich muss entwickelt werden*,[5] the Ego must still evolve. The first sexual satisfactions of an autoerotic nature occur in relation to functions of vital importance. They are based on the satisfaction of the first needs, electing those who care for the child as object choices. Thus, at the outset, the subject "disposes of two sexual objects": himself/herself and the person who takes care of him or her, thereby sedimenting primary narcissism. It is on this basis that Freud introduces the notion of the Ego ideal. If repression proceeds from the Ego, from the regard the Ego has for itself, "we can say that an individual has constructed in himself an ideal in relation to which he measures his own actual Ego."[6] And while the ideal Ego (*Idealich*) speaks to the self-love the real Ego (*wirkliche Ich*) enjoyed in childhood, to the satisfaction of primary narcissism, the Ego ideal (*Ich ideal*) strives to reconquer the lost narcissism, projecting in front of itself its "substitute" as ideal. Freud distinguishes here two functional aspects of the ideal, one imaginary, *Idealich*, the other symbolic, *Ich-ideal*.[7]

Freud elucidates the concepts of identification, first manifestation of an emotional bond with another person, and enamoration, a phenomenon that involves as much an overvaluation of the love object as its idealization, where "a remarkable quantity of narcissistic libido spills over onto the object." "The object is loved by virtue of the perfections that we have targeted for our Ego, and that now, through this indirect path, we wish to procure to satisfy our narcissism."[8] And he concludes: in identification, the object is situated in the Ego's

---

[5] S. Freud, "Zur Einführung des Narzißmus," Gesammelte Werke X, S. Fischer Verlag, Frankfurt, 1991, p. 142.

[6] *Ibid.*, p. 161.

[7] While it is true that in certain contexts Freud seems to use the notions of ideal Ego and Ego ideal interchangeably, in the *Introduction to Narcissism* (*Zur Einführung des Narzißmus, op. cit.*, p. 161) he clearly distinguishes their functions, forming the basis for a precise construction of the identificatory operation. Lacan analyzes this clearly, J. Lacan, *Les écrits techniques de Freud, Le séminaire Livre I*, Editions du Seuil, Paris, 1975, "Idéal du moi et moi ideal", pp. 149-163.

[8] S. Freud, *Massenpsychologie und Ich-Analyse, op. cit.*, p. 124.

place; in enamoration it is situated in the Ego Ideal's place. It is but a step from enamoration to hypnosis, since both involve docility and submission. This is how fascination takes root in a purely narcissistic economy—imaginary, since linked to self-image. While enamoration and fascination involve an intrinsic form of enslavement to the object, the benefit subsists in the narcissistic satisfaction that derives from it. This says a lot about sacrifices for love.

Concerning the mass, Freud concludes his examination with the well-known formulation: it is made up of a certain number of individuals who have put the same object in place of the Ego ideal and who have thus identified with each other in their Ego, which solidifies their libidinal ties, nourishes the force of the mass and allows its members to express affects that otherwise would be inhibited or repressed. Adhesion to it involves a benefit in terms of drive satisfaction.

Individual, Social

The reflection on the libidinal nature of the social tie links social psychology and individual psychology, the political field, and the subjective field. While Lacan was able to say *"l'inconscient, c'est la politique,"* [9] "the unconscious is politics," making radical advances in articulating the subject's connection to the social bond, this question had intensely occupied Freud in his own way. Broached at the time of *Totem and Taboo*, it was addressed again in the post-war writings, from "Considerations on War and Death," through *Group Psychology and the Analysis of the Ego, The Ego and the Id, Civilization and its Discontents, The Future of an Illusion, New Introductory Lessons on Psychoanalysis,* up to the crucial text, *The Man Moses and the Monotheistic Religion.*

In the 1920's Freud was involved in a privileged dialogue on the theme of social structure with the jurist Hans Kelsen, whom he had known since the latter first joined the Vienna Circle in December 1911. War trauma, the end of the Imperial era and the explosion of revolutionary and counter-revolutionary movements led to re-thinking the notion of state and national sovereignty. Freud had published Kelsen's

---

[9] J. Lacan, *La logique du fantasme, Le séminaire Livre XIV* (1966-1967), Éditions du Seuil, Paris, 2023, p. 317.

presentation to the Vienna Psychoanalytic Association, November 30, 1921: "The Conception of State and Social Psychology—With a Special Reference to Freud's Group Theory."[10]

A partisan of positive law as a synthesis of imperative and constraint (*Grundnorme*), of judicial constraint as the expression of the norm's intrinsic validity, Kelsen, in this text, treats the state as a social group, "the most important", he claims, and wonders why a multitude of individuals come to create a unit superior to them, a "super-individual" whole. He is concerned with elucidating the normative and coercive nature of the state. The ad-hoc critique of a series of sociological and psychological theories—Simmel, Le Bon, Durkheim—contrasts with the appreciation of the originality and value of *Massenpsychologie*'s contribution to the comprehension of the nature of the mass. Freud highlights the intrinsic relationship between singular and collective, shows that the consolidation of a "super-individual" social unit, as Kelsen calls it, rests on the projection of a subjective condition; to situate the object in the Ideal Ego's place and identify with the others, deploys a Moebian torsion of the interior toward the exterior and vice-versa, where the subjective object choice consolidates the identification among individuals and sediments the social tie. While the psychological definition of social reality can thus contribute to shedding light on the cohesion proper to the notion of state, the question arises of knowing to what extent the state itself could be considered an example of mass formation, following the characteristics highlighted by Freud. According to Kelsen, Freud would seem inclined to answer this question in the affirmative and he bases his opinion on a particular passage of *Massenpsychologie*: "Everyone is a constitutive element of multiple groups (*Massen*), and—through identification—subject to multilateral ties and has established his own Ego ideal on the basis of the most diverse models. Thus, everyone takes part in numerous group souls (*Massenseelen*), those of race, class, religious community, nation, etc. and can rise above these to achieve a fragment of autonomy and originality."[11]

But Freud has a very different intention. He insists on the plural aspect of subjective identification and on the multilateralism of the

---

[10] Published in English in 1924, *The International Journal of Psychoanalysis* 5, pp. 1-38.

[11] S. Freud, *Massenpsychologie und Ich-Analyse, op. cit.*, p. 144.

social ties that participate in the constitution of the Ego ideal, on the structural relationship between individual and group, on the complex and overdetermined quality of the subjective symbolic universe. At the same time, he stresses the subjection of the individual to the social bond and the way the unconscious is informed by the collective. The process of identification has its foundation in a structural alienation, in taking on as one's own an image found outside of oneself. By virtue of its physiological prematuration, the human offspring's survival requires external care for a much longer period than other mammals, which forces a persistent dependence on the adult. The first immersion in the social bond is the one that occurs in the mother tongue and in the gestures that accompany bodily care. It establishes an encounter between body and speech that revives the drive and inscribes *jouissance*, articulating the first emotional identificatory ties and transmitting at the same time the environment's symbolic rituals. In the contact with the other, the body subjectifies in a signifying manner: the expression of the body is expression of the body/speech, and the symptom—physiological, psychic, or somatic—is the renewed manifestation of their encounter.

If language is metabolized as human substance, this metabolization is always singular, determined by the circumstances relative to the history, the milieu and the culture where the first exchange with the other took place while care was being given. This exchange is inherently a transmission, since the original affective context molds the first identifications with the expectations of those who care for the child and articulates the elements of a cultural background. What we call "culture" is a social tie steeped in the libidinal relationship of the subject with the collective from which it emerges, the echo of which will remain with us for the rest of our life.

Speaking beings thus find themselves both plunged into the collective and marked by identity traits specific to them, particular— particular to their way of responding to the context that concerns them and their way to affect it. But, as Erik Porge points out, these identifying particularities must not be confused with the singularity of the subject, for the foundation of singular identification "resides in the empty box of the unconscious," as Lacan explained. In case it is misunderstood or forgotten "an ordinary particularity is erected as universal and gives rise to what has been called 'the dictatorship (universalization) of identities',"[12] with its diverse forms of segregation.

If Freud uses the word "Massen" to speak about the individual's participation in different collective souls, it is in order to insist on the plurality of imaginary identifications that weave the constitution of the subjective symbolic universe, to stress how much individual psychology is immediately social psychology.

To Believe We are Loved

The Freudian mass has a kind of libidinal compactness around the same object situated in the Ideal's place, around a "One"—virtual, symbolic or real—which is the necessary condition for the organization, the submission and the obedience of numerous individuals. From the place occupied by this One, this ideal, and given its transferential nature (since it is the locus of the object), we are all loved in the same way, says Freud, where the supposition of love is essential to cement the libidinal network that nourishes the mass. In fact, Freud notes that it is absolutely not a panic situation—such as that provoked by a danger—that breaks down the masses' libidinal ties, but rather the loosening of these ties that causes the panic, these panic phenomena typical of the masses' dissolution, for example in the classic case of the loss of the leader. To believe one is loved, to put the object in the ideal's place and shine for it, feeding one's own narcissism, is the key to the "fascination," to that bewitchment which, according to Freud, renders the hypnotic relation identical to a mass formation.

We are all spectators of, or actors in, the fundamental role of fascination at the current stage of the society of the spectacle, where social medias tirelessly exploit the desire to shine in order to leverage narcissism and exhibitionism as well as a fictional feeling of benevolent affiliation, and thus encourage new forms of consumerism and political manipulation. That its intermediary is the image and the imaginary dimension in general, inevitably reminds us that idolatry weds love for meaning, to produce ready-made explanations and the distancing of truth. The use of "likes" speaks volumes on the flattery fed by a system which, in celebrating subjective turgescence—*I like you, I love*

---

[12] E. Porge, "Un malaise dans la psychanalyse," *Essaim* 46, *La psychanalyse et le langage de la guerre*, Editions érès, Toulouse, 2021, p. 14.

you—powers new forms of bewitchment and enslavement. In a January 14, 2021, article, *The New York Times* reported the testimonies of young people who participated in the attack on the U.S Capitol, having arrived in Washington to meet hundreds of followers with the goal of overthrowing the government and overturning the election.[13] A few months earlier, each one of them had tried to attract attention, to create an audience on Facebook. But the bikini photos, the conventional sayings, the intimate revelations, and so on, were unsuccessful. Until the day they decided, each in their own way, to publish radical political content and Trumpian fake news. In a few hours they became *influencers*, submerged under likes, reference points for disparate conspiracy factions, from the partisans of QAnon to the Republican base, to Covid deniers. As one of these young people candidly admits, his only goal in this subversive enterprise was to be accepted, to become popular.

The greater the need to belong to a preestablished identity, the more vulnerable the subject who expresses it. The more a symbolic context is deficient (lack of recognition, affective isolation, segregation, marginalization and so forth) the more there follows a vacillation of the image's stability, of the feeling of self. The adhesion to the mass restores a narcissistic satisfaction and fuels the promise of an agreement, a love for meaning, and for a shared meaning. It matters little if the meaning in question is a complete fallacy.

We know how much Freud reflected on the function of the One. The adoption of the Darwinian hypothesis of the primitive horde subservient to the unlimited authority of a dominant male, the construction of the myth of the primordial father, of the one who can take pleasure from everyone and whose murder becomes necessary, is followed by the creation of a social alliance, where the individual must renounce a good part of his/her own pleasure, instituting at the same time a norm for life in common and an eternal unease, consubstantial with the social contract. It is the One of the logical exception (that *at least one* who does not submit to the phallic function), the dead father by definition, who lays the foundation of a communitarian tie made of obligations and boundaries. While power is originally founded on the

---

[13] S. A. Thompson and C. Warzel, "They used to post selfies. Now they are trying to reverse the election," *The New York Times*, January 14, 2021.

law of the strongest, law emerges from opposition to the excessive power of the individual in order to represent the force of the community, a force which nevertheless always continues to use violence, ready to be unleashed against any opposition. According to Freud, the social alliance is an unstable formation, always susceptible to being threatened, from the inside as well as the outside and it rests on two elements: coercion and identificatory links among its members. "The community must be permanently maintained, organize itself, establish regulations which prevent dangerous insurrections, create institutions that watch over the enforcement of regulations—of laws—and that ensure the execution of acts of violence in accordance with the laws"[14]-since law itself requires a form of violence. The social alliance, in its most elementary as well as its most highly articulated forms, includes a structural tension.

According to the libidinal unit that defines it, the mass presents itself instead as a cohesive and potentially stable formation—think of the army or the church. This isn't the case with the social alliance as Freud sees it, naturally unstable, necessarily bearing the mark of the lack, of a perpetual and intrinsic drive limitation—which delineates, in response to Kelsen, a structural difference between mass and state. One might wonder to what extent in certain totalitarian regimes the state may model a mass formation, that doesn't however exhaust the complexity of the social bond where such a mass resides. The very fact that it is based on a libidinal logic that calls upon Eros as the principal for union, upon the One, the notion of mass "entifies,"[15] as Lacan notes, the idea of the 'whole,' which marks its imaginary dimension and represents the illusion that something can exist like a desired and self-sufficient completeness. This phantasmatic feeling of the whole is precisely what gives the mass a captivating and effective power, and a certain exaltation, similar to that of enamoration, with all the consequences relative to the dark side of passion, such as hatred and

---

[14] S. Freud, "Warum Krieg?" Gesammelte Werke XVI, S. Fischer Verlag, Frankfurt, 1950, pp. 19-20. "Community must be maintained permanently, must be organized, must draw up regulations to anticipate the risk of rebellion and must institute authorities to see that those regulations – the laws – are respected and to superintend the execution of legal acts of violence." Freud, "Why War?", *The Standard Edition of the Works of Sigmund Freud*, Vol. XXII, p. 205.

[15] J. Lacan, ...*ou pire, Le séminaire Livre XIX*, Éditions du Seuil, Paris, 2011, p. 167.

destructiveness. The illusion of the One is the logical motor of the exclusion of the other, the exterior, the enemy, a necessary element to consolidate the mass's identity.

Nevertheless, this entification of the mass, efficient as it is, is more apparent than real, or better, is only one of its facets. As Lacan has suggested, the *Massenpsychologie* misses "the nature of the *not all* that founds it." [16] The unary trait, which is the mark of the primary identification of the ideal, is the trait of difference, it founds repetition, and repetition can never create a "whole." Moreover, Freud stresses that the crowd inherits its nature from the horde. The horde is founded on the father's exception. The myth of the *Urvater*—of the One who enjoyed all women—is rooted in the logical function of the exception, on the basis that there is "at least one" who avoids castration. [17] It is from the One, from the missing One, that a structural asymmetry appears between sexual partners—an impossible, that targets the real of the incompleteness in *jouissances.* "Like Janus, the crowd is two-faced," [18] as Porge puts it. One of its sides derives from a logic of the whole, the other from a logic of the *not all*, a duplicity that blazes trails to shake up from the inside every social discourse that feeds on the totalitarianism of the One.

The mass describes one of the collective formations in the social tie. Lacan clearly shows that, once the temporal dimension of haste is introduced in the social synchrony, the collective from which the subject emerges does not rest on an identity among its members. The emergence of the subject of the assertion, of an assertion of the type "I am white" (or black, or good, or sad and so on) involves the passage through an indefinite subject and a reciprocal subject, logical instances within the collective. [19] The certainty that animates the time to conclude implies a de-identifying de-subjectification that allows for acting. In the collective order, the relation between individuals is determined by the subjective division this relation establishes, which is based on

---

[16] *Ibid.*

[17] J. Lacan, *Encore, Le séminaire Livre XX*, Éditions du Seuil, Paris, 1975, pp. 73-82.

[18] See E. Porge, *Truth and Knowledge in the Clinic, Working with Freud and Lacan*, The Sea Horse Imprint, Agincourt Press, New York, 2016, p. 152.

[19] As Lacan articulates in his "Logical Time and the Assertion of Anticipated Certainty," in *Écrits, The First Complete Edition in English*, trans. Bruce Fink, Norton & Company, New York and London, 2007.

the inadequate nature of the relationship between the one and the Other, particular to the reciprocal relation. This involves a new way of counting, which reflects the fact that "the collective is none other than the subject of the individual."[20]

Of the Superego

Following, among other things, his dialog with Kelsen and the observations the latter made regarding the *Massenpsychologie*, Freud deepens his reflection on the relationship between the subject and the collective, emphasizing his distance from Kelsen's idealistic belief on the nature of the law. He formulates a theory encompassing the functional and metapsychological value of the Superego.[21] The fundamental question is that of understanding what leads us to obey and prevents us from rebelling against constraints—a question that is destined, among other effects, "to explode" the fictive self-sufficiency of Kelsen's *Grundnorme*.[22] In fact, this is a crucial question, that ties together social scene and subjective scene, and that establishes an intrinsic contact between law and psychoanalysis, between the field of law and the field of drives. As Freud never tires of repeating, there would be no law without the drive.

The child's vulnerability makes it such that catering to need is combined with a demand for love that forces the child to submit to the parent's will: *"Das Kind unter dem Zwange stand,"*[23] a primary constraint where survival itself is at stake and that sediments the first identifications, the internalization of adults' desires and their law. But, as Freud points out, the Superego that derives from it is the fruit of an injunction and an interdiction at the same time: "Be like your father, don't be like your father," the source of a structural impossibility, of an

---

[20] *Ibid.*, p. 175. This new way of counting is the one Lacan defines as *One plus a*, see his February 16, 1973 lesson in *Encore, Le séminaire Livre* XX, Éditions du Seuil, Paris, 1975.

[21] The term 'Superego' is introduced for the first time in *The Ego and the Id*. Yet, the roots of its function had already been identified by Freud while exploring censorship and the relation between Ideal Ego and Ego Ideal in "Introduction to Narcissism" (*Zur Einführung des Narzißmus*), *op. cit.*, p. 162.

[22] E. Balibar, "Freud et Kelsen, 1922. L'invention du surmoi," *Incidence 3, Le surmoi, genèse politique*, Editions Michel de Maule, Paris, Octobre 2007.

[23] S. Freud, *Das Ich und das Es*, Gesammelte Werke XIII, S, Fischer Verlag, Frankfurt, 1987, pp. 277-278.

antinomy that condemns the subject to both transgression and guilt. A linear way of internalizing the law of the Other does not exist; the inevitable feeling of guilt is the primarily unconscious affect that signals the Ego's subjection to the Superego. Freud's famous and precious clinical observation resides here: namely, that the feeling of unconscious guilt precedes the crime, or rather, that far from being its cause, in many cases the crime is the effect of an unconscious guilt. Acting in reality gives a semblance of motivation to the relentlessness of the guilt, lightening its unexplained load by giving it a reason, so to speak. Perhaps it is also because of this that on the horizon of religious mythology the fault's motive always lacks sense; whether apples or plums are involved, the crime is always incongruous relative to the fault.

In the psychic tribunal where differentiated roles are enacted— accused and accuser, executioner and victim—the fault-punishment circuit condemns the Ego masochistically to an incessant punishment and servitude, which is at the same time an incessant source of *jouissance*. The servile solution allows saving one's skin but also taking pleasure as much from a supposed love as from assured punishment. Thus, the clinic shows that the patients are the servants of their own sickness and, something that Freud repeatedly insists on, that they find a drive satisfaction in the symptom and in their own suffering, refusing to give up on the punishment that feeds guilt. This is one of the major resistances to treatment—all the more evident in the contemporary clinic, marked as it is by today's primacy of obsessional neurosis.

Originally conceived of by Freud as the inheritor of the decomposition of the Oedipal complex and the primary identification with the father figure, the Superego takes the shape of a repressive and punitive authority that condenses not only the relation to the authority of parents and those who replace them, but also with the other authorities encountered in the social link, teachers, coaches, mentors, and so on. This palimpsest of the subjective experience of constraint ties the subjective to the collective. And that is not all. It becomes the bearer of the group's experience as it relates to law and tradition, the vehicle of a transmission of the norm between generations. Freud stresses that, when they educate the child, the parents and their substitutes obey the injunctions of their own Superego; "In fact, the child's Superego is not built according to its parents' model, but according to their Superego; it takes on the same content, it becomes the vehicle of tradition, of all the enduring value judgements that have been transmitted like this from generation to generation."[24] The obedience, the difficulty of rebelling against constraint, are woven into the emergence of the subject from the collective, into the symbolic debt contracted with the communities to which the subject belongs. But it is a symbolic debt that conveys precise modalities of *jouissance*, carrying the real in the passage of generations.

Concerning the genealogy of the Superego, Freud insists on something at once obvious and crucial: the fact that the Superego, like the Ego, "originates in things heard."[25] The language that inscribes the signifying structure institutes the dimension of law. "The first utterance decrees, legislates, aphorizes, is oracle, it confers on the real other its obscure authority."[26] From the adult, the newborns receive the first sign of their relationship with the Other, the *unary trait as* Lacan calls it, that registers the weight of what is said in the field of the Other. The first utterance is directive and enigmatic, yet to be deciphered. It will engender the belief that from its decoding depends one own's existence and survival, one's own chance to be loved. The child questions this utterance, questions the very nature of discourse and its function in the place of the Other—a place from which the subject is situated as subject of speech.

In essence, the superego "is speech itself, the commandment of the law, inasmuch as only the root of it remains."[27] It embodies the most reduced function of language, naked speech as pure imperative—in which its enigmatic and terrifying aspect is undiminished. It is speech as law, a law one believes it needs to be obeyed.

If we think of the tonalities of Mussolini's declarations, of his emphasis on adverbs and conjunctions to the detriment of nouns and content, of the words screamed or vomited from Hitler's throat, or of Trump's syntactic gibberish—whose vocabulary is limited to fifty words—if we consider the acclamations, the success with which they were met, we might well wonder to what extent the imperative pho-

---

[24] S. Freud, *Neue Folge Vorlsungen zur Einführung in die Psychoanalyse*, Gesammelte Werke XIV, S. Fischer Verlag, Frankfurt, 1990, p. 73.

[25] S. Freud, *Das Ich und das Es, op. cit.*, p. 282.

[26] J. Lacan, "Subversion du sujet et dialectique du désir," in *Écrits*, Éditions du Seuil, Paris, 1966, p. 808.

[27] J. Lacan, *Les écrits techniques de Freud, Le séminaire Livre I*, Éditions du Seuil, Paris, 1975, p. 119.

nemes of speech evoke the original sideration through which we are subjugated by naked speech, becoming instruments of submission and fascination. In human language "the sender receives its own message from the receiver in an inverted form,"[28] according to a mirroring effect which inverts the positions of the speaker and the listener. The dictates of the Superego ("you must," "you are," "be"... etc.), their imperative and assertive nature, are imbued with the fabric of the one who receives them.

Freud notes that the Superego answers to everything we expect to be "the most elevated" in nature. As a substitutive formation of the desired father (*Vatersehnsucht*), it contains the seed from which all religions are born."[29] This desired father—the other side of the feared and persecuting father—this joyful, tender father that Alyosha Karamazov rediscovers while praising God,[30] this loving father summoned in inner reflection, emerges from the very act of speech. As Lacan stresses, the signifier requires the establishment of a place that is other, the place of the Other, of the Other *as witness*—witness of the partners in a dialog and condition for speech to be able to establish the dimension of truth. At speech's horizon, the Other necessarily emerges as the location of truth. "As long as words are said, the hypothesis of God will be there."[31]

If subjection is intrinsically associated with the nature of the speaking being, with the economy of the drives that regulates language, with the legislating Other who marks the emergence of the subject, then the question is raised of knowing what is the margin of subjective autonomy and freedom—the margin of *reconquest* and transformation of what was inherited from our own parents, in order to make of it something of our own and recognize that the law that binds one generation to the other can be renegotiated. This points to an ethical and therefore political direction for psychoanalysis.

---

[28] J. Lacan, "Fonction et champ de la parole et du langage en psychanalyse," in *Écrits*, Éditions du Seuil, Paris, 1966, p. 298.

[29] S. Freud, *Das Ich und das Es, op. cit.*, p. 265.

[30] Alexei Fyodorovich Karamazov, F. Dosto[y]evsky, *The Brothers Karamazov*, Vol. 3, Chapter 11.

[31] J. Lacan, *Encore, Le séminaire Livre XX*, Éditions du Seuil, Paris, 1975, p. 44.

A Direction

At the origin of the three main reasons mentioned by La Boétie to shed light on the disturbing question of voluntary servitude, as well as the fascination exerted by the One—habit, *panem et circenses*, and the tyrannical pyramid—there is the theme of *jouissance*. Habit is based on the insistence of the same sources of pleasure, which involves compulsion, resistance to change, repetition, as well as the persistence of suffering in the form of symptoms and the drive satisfaction related to them. *Panem et circenses*, the carnivalesque parentheses conceded to the people by the tyrant, was a celebration of every excess—games, abundance of food, participation in the enjoyment of killing, voyeurism etc.—and it marvelously reinforced the powers that be, as did the illusion of serving an intermittently benevolent regime. It is worth asking, *mutatis mutandis*, what points in common these practices have with today's media spectacles; consider the obscenity and sadism of *"The Apprentice, The ultimate job interview in the ultimate jungle"*—where the term "jungle" perfectly describes the attitude of current neoliberalism—which earned Trump celebrity, money and above all a large electoral base. The tyrannical pyramid also rests on opportunism and *jouissance*. The tyrant's direct servants cultivate his favor with the aim of obtaining specific advantages. The same applies to the hundreds of people who serve them, and so on and so forth, until the lowest rank where we find those who gain only suffering and servitude from their advantages. Naturally, the pyramid shows that the flip side of the will to serve is the will to dominate.

While in the domain of political philosophy, utility, opportunism, and the will to dominate consolidate the structures of servitude, for Freud the intrinsic relation between law and violence takes place in the domain of the drive. As he asserts in his dialog with Einstein about war, aggressive tendencies dictated by the death drive, expressed internally or externally, cannot be eliminated, nor can the erotic drives that establish ties of love or identification, including those that undergird group psychology, its illusory aspect, and the paranoid and segregationist reactions it can engender. The drive's fusion is intrinsic to the libido and to the death drive characteristic of the speaking being. Yet, Freud sees in the evolution of *Kultur* a transformation of the modalities of coercion, coupled with a progressive restriction of the drive vicissitudes which accompanies the discontents characteristic of "civilization." At the same time, he points out the singular process which, starting with the manifestation of new ideal, ethic and esthetic exigencies can transform subjective violence and lead to its "constitutional intolerance."[32] What makes someone rebel against war given that for as long as the world has existed there have always been wars, since they are part of interhuman commerce? The verb Freud uses is *empören*,[33] to be overcome by a feeling of indignation, an affect that is the expression of a new drive economy, but which is also the motor of another possibility of action of the singular in the collective. Sublimation is central to it.

It is interesting to observe how the practice of the unconscious, one worthy of the name, leads to a form of sensitizing, of a putting into continuity our own condition and the alterity from which it emerges and with which it is in relation. If indignation surfaces, for example against violence, injustice, the gratuity of evil or destruction, it isn't through a spirit of compassion nor, as Spinoza views it, because of a feeling of likeness with our fellow humans dictated by the faculty of imagination. It comes, rather, from the effect of a practice, of lengthy work, based on the recognition of the subjective division and the assumption of the separation between truth and knowledge. It is the effect of a stripping away, first of all of the idolatry of the Ego and the illusions fed by the Ideal, of a decentering of the feeling of self; it is the effect of frequenting the real, which voids the passion for ignorance and progressively deposes the Subject Supposed to Know—that is its counterpart—also voiding the accompanying servitudes of love. If the passion for ignorance is a vehicle for the transference, and the transference is a form of love, since we love the one who is supposed to know, the transference can surely contribute to the tribune from which we believe we are loved and admired, as in the case of suggestion or of love of the Master; but also, in the case of the identification to the analyst. But, as Freud states, in the analytical act, the transference is instrument and obstacle, destined for its own dissolution, destined precisely for the fall of the Subject Supposed to Know. In the act, the attribution of knowledge to the Other accompanies the repeated encounter with the structural incommensurability between truth and

---

[32] S. Freud, *Warum Krieg? op.cit.*, p. 26.

[33] *Empören*: the transitive means "to outrage," the reflexive means "to rise up," "to rebel out of indignation."

knowledge and goes in the direction of the deconstruction of the One toward the *not-all*, toward challenging all appealing illusions.

This is how the political value of the act takes shape, as well as the importance, on the terrain of any analytical practice worthy of the name, of the conceptualization of the end of analysis and its crucial role in the analyst's formation. For such an end to take place, there needs to be an analyst who can conduct and sustain it, an analyst who has had the experience of the end of one own's personal analysis and who is able to bring an analysis to its end, an analyst who situates her or his act from the place of the object *a*, as defined by Lacan, and who does not choose to occupy the position of the Subject Supposed to Know—which revives suggestion. This means respecting both the time of analysis and the time of formation, which are always singular, always subjective, and making a distinction between the moment the analysand begins to practice and the moment corresponding to the end of his/her analysis. At the collapse of the attribution of knowledge to the analyst, the analysand who begins to practice responds with a singular act of faith: s/he institutes himself/herself as Subject Supposed to Know, and in so doing, s/he identifies with the *"sujet de la tromperie…"*, "the subject of trickery," as Lacan defines it.[34] This involves a moment of the cure that calls up an ulterior logical time, when this renewed belief will be challenged.

To dwell in seduction, mastery or trickery, is to consolidate and reinforce the tyrannical pyramid—as we so often see in the effects of the current ideologizing performances of little masters and professors.

Wo Es war, soll Ich werden, Freud writes. "There where it was [...] it's my duty that I come to be,"[35] translates Lacan. Both trace a specific ethical itinerary which, starting from the recognition and the assumption of the subjective division attributes to the subject the possibility of becoming, of *trans-forming* itself, of passing from a position of *alieni iuris* to one of *sui iuris*. By deconstructing the mystifying function of group and individual identifications and they related norms, by reappropriating one own's heritage to turn it into the material from which a new and singular voice emerges, analytic practice

---

[34] J. Lacan, *Problèmes cruciaux pour la psychanalyse, Le séminaire Livre XII*, 1964-1965, unpublished, May 19, 1965 session.

[35] J. Lacan, "La chose freudienne ou Sens du retour à Freud en psychanalyse" in *Écrits*, Paris, Éditions du Seuil, 1966, pp. 417-418.

may return to the individual the subjective responsibility for her or his own choices, her or his own actions—which also allows participating differently in the collective reality to which one belongs. It allows summoning the "author" in us—in its original meaning of *auctor*, from the Latin *augeo.* "In its earliest usages, *augeo* indicates not the fact of increasing what exists but of producing from own's own breast," [36] as Benveniste points out with finesse. The notion of *auctor* yields many different usages, but it is clearly linked to the original meaning of *augeo*, "to bring out, to promote." It is this meaning that is found in the early notion of *auctoritas*: an utterance that determines and brings about a change in the world, un utterance capable of "making something emerge and—literarily—to produce existence."[37]

In this sense, the irreducibility of the individual unconscious proves to be a beneficial factor of disparity and social resistance, a factor of disintegration of the discourse of subjugation, thus blazing a militant and ethical trail for the political unconscious.

(Translated by Jacques Houis)

---

[36] E. Benveniste, *Le vocabulaire des institutions indo-européennes, tome 2, Pouvoir, droit, religion*, Les éditions de Minuit, Paris, 1969, p. 149.

[37] *Ibid.*, p. 151.

Betty Bernardo Fuks is a psychoanalyst practicing in Rio de Janeiro. She holds a PhD in Communication and Culture (Federal University of Rio de Janeiro) and she is Professor in the Postgraduate Program in Psychoanalysis, Health, and Society at University Veiga de Almeida (Rio de Janeiro). The author of numerous articles on psychoanalysis, her books include: *Freud e a cultura and Freud e a judeidade*, published in English as *Freud and the Invention of Jewishness, O Homem Moisés e a religião monoteísta, o desvelar de um assassinato.*

Paola Mieli is a psychoanalyst practicing in New York City and president of Après-Coup Psychoanalytic Association (New York). The author of numerous essays on psychoanalysis and on culture, her books include: *Figures of Space. Subject, Body, Place*; *A Silver Martian--Normality and Segregation in Primo Levi's Sleeping Beauty in the Fridge*; *Sobre as manipulaçaões irreversíveis do corpo.*

Rosalind C. Morris is an anthropologist and cultural critic. She is Professor of Anthropology at Columbia University. Her books include: *Unstable Ground: The Lives, Deaths, and Afterlives of Gold in South Africa; The Returns of Fetishism: Charles de Brosses and the Afterlives of an Idea;* and *Accounts and Drawing from Underground*, with William Kentridge. She is the author of many essays on art, social media, and politics.

David Pavón-Cuéllar is Professor of Marxism, Social Psychology and Psychoanalysis at the *Universidad Michoacana de San Nicolás de Hidalgo*, Morelia, Mexico. His books include: *Psychoanalysis and revolution: critical psychology for liberation movements*, with Ian Parker; *Marxism and Psychoanalysis, in or against Psychology?; Lacan, Discourse, Event. New Psychoanalytic Approaches to Textual Indeterminacy;* and *From the Conscious Interior to an Exterior Unconscious: Lacan, Discourse Analysis and Social Psychology.*

Alain Vanier is a psychoanalyst and psychiatrist, and an emeritus professor at the Université Paris VII Diderot. He is member and past president of Espace Analytique (Paris) and a faculty member at Après-Coup Psychoanalytic Association. In English translation, the Other Press has published his monograph *Lacan.*

Titles Published by The Sea Horse Imprint:

Betty Bernardo Fuks — *Freud and the Invention of Jewishness* (2008)

Gérard Haddad — *Eating the Book: Dietary Rites and Paternal Function* (2013)

Erik Porge — *Truth and Knowledge in the Clinic: Working with Freud and Lacan* (2016)

Paola Mieli — *Figures of Space: Subject, Body, Place* (2017)

Alain Didier-Weill — *The Three Times of the Law* (2017)

Marie-Magdeleine Lessana — *Marilyn: Portrait of a Shooting Star* (2019)

Jean-Pierre Cléro — *Lacan and the English Language* (2020)

Patrick Landman — *Are We All Hyperactive? The Astonishing Epidemic of Attention Disorders* (2024)

Gisèle Chaboudez — *The Feminine Deal* (2024)

Betty Bernardo Fuks, Paola Mieli, Rosalind Morris, David Pavón-Cuéllar, Alain Vanier — *Then and Now: On the Crowd, the Subject, and the Collective* (2024)

www.ingramcontent.com/pod-product-compliance
Lightning Source LLC
Chambersburg PA
CBHW032055040426
42335CB00037B/772